THE PARTICIPATIVE PRINCE

Techniques for developing your organization

and improving its performance

by

Daniel A. Tagliere

To the princes and princesses of organization pyramids everywhere who are more concerned with performance and productivity than personal power ... and to their consultants.

THE PARTICIPATIVE PRINCE

Techniques for developing your organization

and improving its performance

by

Daniel A. Tagliere

ODS Publications, Inc.
444 N. Michigan Avenue
Chicago, Illinois 60611 U.S.A.

CHICAGO RESEARCH AND TRADING GROUP, LTD.
440 SOUTH LA SALLE STREET
CHICAGO, ILLINOIS 60605

ODS Publications, Inc.

International standard book number 0-9602516-0-X

Library of Congress catalog card number 79-83886

First printing, 1980.

SALUTATION

To the Princes and Princesses of the Pyramid:

This book is primarily directed to you who have position power in your organizations. I think of you as princes and princesses because I find myself identifying with Niccolo Machiavelli who wrote for the powerful and would-be powerful in his classic, The Prince. Niccolo, of course, wrote with a real prince in mind, Lorenzo de' Medici, the 16th century ruler of Florence. Similarly, I am writing for real people with real power who can have their way in their organizations or in a segment of it. In this sense, Niccolo's purpose and mine are similar and I hope you find this book a clear, non-judgmental approach to certain ends as is The Prince. I also hope that there my identification with Machiavelli ends.

The Prince is a treatise on how rulers can acquire and keep political power. While Niccolo hoped that Lorenzo would use his power to serve the cause of the state, he knew that power must be obtained before it can be used. He also knew that power is not really power if the prince can't opt to use it for his own ends rather than for the state.

Lest you think me naive, let me say at this point that I know that most people who have power are people who have a relatively high need for it, and therefore do the things necessary to achieve it. And once they have it, they become so attached to it that they give it up only with great reluctance.

This would seem to imply that the audience for this book is small---either for those with power who do not have a strong psychological need for it, or those who are sufficiently secure to risk losing it, or are willing to further the goals of the organization even at the expense of their personal power to control the organization. The latter group is no doubt my primary target audience because I believe such princes and princesses, with established participative tendencies, will be most receptive to my words.

But allow me a small effort to convince those who see their position in the organization as a vehicle for filling their power need. To these majesties I would say that I offer no moral argument to convince you to put the organization's needs above your own. Your needs, your views and your goals may be more righteous, virtuous and correct and only you can make that judgment. You may need your power to curb the organization from committing wrong, stupid, or even heinous acts. I offer no opinions on issues in this work. The arguments I offer regarding putting the organization interests above your own are these:

1.   While giving small powers away may feel uncomfortable and the risk of losing more is real, the actual casualties in terms of status and ultimate control are few.

2.   The success of the organization will almost always result in the success of those with power in it.

3.   While giving up power may seem uncomfortable and inhibiting---like braces for teeth or bones---it may actually provide greater freedom and strength in the long run.

4.   The risks involved in sharing power can be tried in small ways and can usually be retracted if the results seem wrong.

This book then, is for you who have real power resulting from your rank in the organization, whether you are participative or directive in style. To a lesser extent, this book is also addressed to those with different kinds of power such as that derived from special expertise, experiences, or charisma. These individuals, while they are relatively powerless to initiate the use of the ideas and techniques I offer, can introduce them to the truly powerful, encourage them to try the ideas and support their efforts when they do. For simplicity's sake, I have chosen to write in the first person singular directly to those who have subordinates in an organization. In other words, to the person of top level organization rank who can do what he or she wishes with the organization under his or her control. However, much of the material will also be useful to those of lesser rank in the organization who manage others.

Similarly, much of the message of this book is applicable to all types of organizations: families, representative bodies, school boards, play groups, and so on. However, the types of organizations most in my mind as I write are those commonly known as hierarchical or pyramid organizations. These are organizations where one or a small number of persons are most powerful and distribute power downward through one or more echelons of subordinates. This type of organization is, and has been throughout human history, most widely used for political, military, religious, business and other types of organizations.

There has been considerable talk in recent years about scrapping the pyramid model of organizations. Those who would like to see it laid aside claim that it doesn't adequately picture a manager's job; much of the manager's work is outside the realm of dealing with subordinates and superiors.

Others feel the pyramid is outdated because some progressive companies have adopted so-called "matrix" organizations. This means that a person may be under the direct authority of two or even three people and may share power over subordinates. This type of organization definitely has a future. Use of the matrix will grow, but it will probably never amount to more than a fraction of one percent of the number of pyramid organizations. Also, it may be argued that the matrix concept usually is operational in only portions of large organizations that are actually pyramid organizations.

In some organizations the pyramid is retained but the organization chart is not used. In such organizations there are executives and there are workers, but the relative status of every manager in between is kept intentionally vague. No organization charts are published so most members of the organization can only become familiar with the power relationships of those they come in contact with.

Proponents of the unpublished chart model usually proudly describe their organization as informal. They claim that informality inhibits buck passing and the "not-my-job" syndrome. They also claim that informality better enables the "mover," "wheeler dealer," and "high achiever" to do his or her thing---to get the job done without being inhibited by the bureaucracy. Bureaucracies, they claim, start with organization charts.

Obviously there is some truth to these views but they do not ring the death knell for pyramid organizations. The traditional charts may go and individuals may find themselves able to move about the pyramid for short-term assignments, but power---the need for it, the struggle for it, and the value placed on it---is here to stay. And where there is power, whether it is structurally ordained or the every-person-for-him-or-herself variety, there is an open or hidden hierarchical or pyramid organization.

Pyramid organizations have long proven their worthiness in times of crisis and war. Military organizations are usually the epitome of the pyramid model. This no doubt evolved as soon as ancient man realized that a disciplined force under a single head was more effective than the shaky collaboration of individual warriors. Speedy decision making, implementation, and control of resources are essential to success in battle and other military situations.

Architectural pyramids, such as those of ancient Egypt and ancient America, make very durable structures and have become symbols of stability and strength.

Perhaps these characteristics of architectural pyramids are also the basic reasons for the durability of organizational pyramids.

Most of us seem to have a natural identification with pyramid organizations. Since most of us were raised in families directed by a powerful parent figure, we readily assimilate into pyramid organizations. Clear lines of authority show us to whom we should be submissive and to whom we can be more dominant. Because pyramid organizations promote stability and predictability, they give us a feeling of security. And security is what most of us seem to want most of the time. Pyramid organizations will be around for a long time to come, as long as they provide control for those with power and security for those without.

The problem with traditional pyramid organizations is that they tend to promote a closed, tomb-like atmosphere where good talents lie mummified and buried. They tend to inhibit the free exchange of ideas, the development of new ideas, and the solving of problems. In such organizations, problem solving is the province of the powerful. Decision making is at the top and executed downward---from the brains to the limbs. Communication is also mostly downward with little going upward or sideways.

Pyramid organizations traditionally expect the powerful members to make decisions on their own. They also expect the lower echelon members to follow out the orders of the powerful. In so doing, many people and their talents are underutilized. A manufacturing organization that wouldn't dream of purchasing a high priced, complex piece of machinery and then let it lay idle when it could be producing will think nothing of using only a small portion of the capacity of its human resources.

Human beings are resources that can create ideas, solve problems, and serve as sensors and conduits of useful information, as well as do more mechanical jobs. Nonetheless, people are told in a great number of overt and covert ways not to use their full capacities. They are told that their brains are to function only to the extent necessary to carry out their assignments. Usually assignments are limited to functional applications of concepts developed by some mastermind. The sad part of this underutilization, beyond the fact that the organization is not optimally successful, is that most people, however low on the pyramid, want to help their organizations succeed. They identify with its success and are willing and able to be further utilized. What's more, they will do so proudly for no additional compensation.

While underutilization may be acceptable and even desirable in organizations where the goals and strategies are relatively simple and easily comprehended by a few leaders, it can be disastrous to the complex organization. Complex here means that the problems, procedures, policies, and opportunities are too complex for one or even an entire elite clan to comprehend and run in a directive fashion.

The question is, how can we maintain the pyramid and thereby keep all of its advantages while we also more fully utilize the great power of the human members who care about the organization's continuing success? As the saying goes, how can we "have our cake and eat it, too?"

The problem of the pyramid, like the riddle of the sphinx, can be solved. It is possible to have both structure and freedom. The organization can be a vehicle or conduit for the personal growth of its members. It doesn't have to be a prison. The talents of the members can be more fully used while the pyramid endures, even grows stronger, more durable, more stable and more successful.

So, dear princes and princesses of pyramids everywhere, please read on. I know that most of you, should you have children, would like to see them grow and prosper, even if it is at the expense of your own control over them. I also know that at times you feel the same about your organizations. When you do, you will want ideas on how you can accomplish these goals. This is what I offer here.

THANK YOU

There is nothing that can be accomplished alone. This book is no exception. Besides the countless contributors to the growing body of knowledge centering on the human organization, I would specifically like to thank the following:

For editorial review:

Margaret Ann Tagliere
Harry Tankus
David and Bernadette Jahns
Richard and Irma Bartels
Pat Jordan

For manuscript, art and production contribution:

Pauline Eck
Irene Mc Namee
Dennis Miller
Vivian E. Sheppard

CONTENTS

come resistance from within and
without - judgment, when to lead
and when to follow.

Definitions - organization diagnosis -
management by objectives - team
building or group development -
value analysis - contracting - mission
statement - long range planning -
attitude surveys - org development -
behavior modification - norm modification - job enrichment or job
enlargement - sociotechnical redesign -
force field analysis - conflict
resolution - intergroup merging -
interpersonal feedback - OD team
development - multiple management -
training - sales organization - sales
group development and group selling -
internal consultant development -
organization planning - human
resource planning - brainstorming -
PERT - planned meetings - career
planning - labor/management
committees - information systems
analysis - troubled employee
programs - quality of work life.

One-on-one relationships: leader/
follower, most powerful/least
powerful, specialist/user -
individual/group relationships -
intragroup relationships - intergroup relationships.

OD groups - purpose - development -
membership - mission - problem or
project content - work setting -
structure - meeting procedures:
performance or productivity
improvement, creative problem
solving, corrective problem solving -
preventive problem solving, project
planning, proposal development, proposal evaluation - communication
skills - processes: negative,
positive - further suggestions.

For developing individuals - for
developing client/consultant
relationships - for developing
one-on-one relationships - for
training and developing groups -
for developing a network of
groups and intergroup relationships - for developing organization diagnostic data.

CHAPTER 1

ABOUT ORGANIZATIONS AND PRODUCTIVITY

To begin, it is essential for you to understand the theoretical basis upon which I have built the more specific techniques and strategies presented in later chapters.

First, let me tell you how I define organization. An organization is two or more persons interacting within a mutually recognized power relationship for some common purpose. As you can see, this definition is broad enough to cover everything from a two-person barbershop to a giant industrial or governmental organization. And, it should be broad. They are all organizations and by any definition should have something in common to qualify for the name.

There are numerous ways to identify and classify organizations to fit many different purposes. For example, some people think of them poetically, as carriages or cages. To one person, the organization is a wondrous vehicle that can transport him/her to great heights of fame, wealth, power, and fulfillment. Of course, he/she must have the power, know how, and the opportunity to influence what the organization does. To others the organization is a cage that inhibits movements, controls thoughts and feelings, and generally limits self fulfillment.

Another way to look at organizations in a poetic philosophic sense is to see them as devices for expressing ideas. Religions, political entities and commercial enterprises all started with ideas and took form in order to express them. Interestingly enough, the organizations seem more often than not to adopt the nature of their human creators. Ultimately they become more concerned with survival than anything else. They want to live on even after their usefulness is gone and even if it means behaving in direct opposition to the basic ideals on which they were founded. But on to more practical matters.

Many people think of organizations in terms of their size: number of members, budget, or sales volume. Others think of them by their function, such as caring for the elderly or manufacturing milling machines. Still others just classify them under headings like industrial, governmental, educational, health care, social, etc. I would like to suggest that for purposes of following the message of this book you think of organizations in terms of member participation. Picture a straight-line continuum representing the extent to which the members of the organization share in determining the purpose of the organization and its goals, identifying the problems and opportunities it faces, and making decisions regarding how its resources will be used.

At one extreme on our continuum would be the organization where the leader makes all decisions regarding mission, strategy, policies, and procedures of the organization with little or no input from other members. At the other extreme on the continuum would be organizations where every member is involved in the decision making processes.

Does position on this continuum always correlate with performance or productivity? I would like to say unequivocally yes; yes the greater the participation the higher the productivity. But I cannot. Can it be proven that greater participation always correlates with higher morale? Again, I cannot attest to that. Nor can I say that leaders who operate with a very high degree of control are ineffective, unliked or dictatorial in manner.

I know of many such leaders who run highly productive organizations in a positive paternal manner. Despite this fact I recommend more participation in most work organizations. Why? Because to make paternalism work several difficult-to-integrate factors are necessary. First, it requires a highly control-oriented leader with the intelligence, energy, and time to oversee every detail of the organization. The leader must also be perceived by those working for him as a strong figure who inspires loyalty and devotion. Such an organization also must have members who like working under the guidance and control of a strong leader who always knows what to do and how to do it. The organization itself must be on the small side and its operations highly routine and carefully structured so the leader can maintain control. The problem solving that the people who work in this type of organization engage in must largely be limited to corrective or preventive in nature. They probably wouldn't deal with creative problem solving because their job is to keep the organization "machine" running by keeping their "cog" functioning.

There are and perhaps always will be organizations like this and the kind of leader who can control them and make them highly productive. However, the growing complexities of even small organizations and the individualistic attitudes of increasing number of leaders and followers indicate a long term trend toward more participative leadership.

Now about productivity. It must be defined. While it may be difficult to define productivity in specific situations, it is no more difficult to define in a general way than it is to define organization. For our purposes, productivity is that which an organization accomplishes and that can be measured. For some organizations it is quite easy to identify and measure productivity. Manufacturing is the first example that comes to mind, but any organization that can easily identify what it produces or accomplishes and what it costs to operate can quickly measure its progress or lack of it in terms of productivity.

If your organization is one of the many staff or service units that reacts to the needs of line departments you know it is more difficult to measure what your organization does. This can be a comforting thing or a nuisance depending on your own psychological needs and the politics of your situation. In either case, you must accept the fact that without measurability, your feeling of accomplishment must be just that---a feeling. Regardless of how widespread the good feelings are about your organization's progress or contribution, you can never know if the principles in this book, or in any book on efficiency and productivity are working. In this book I talk mostly of practical things that not only can be accomplished, but that can be proven and communicated in a clear, unambiguous manner. Any compromise with the measurability requirement must be considered a weakness, so you will eventually have to come to grips with what productivity means in your organization.

Now that the key definitions have been expressed, let me tell you what I'm hoping you will have when you finish reading this chapter.

First, I hope that you are more strongly convinced than ever before that productivity is the key issue in all organizations. As you will see, my focus and frame of reference is that of work organizations, but even family organizations produce such things as member support, comfort, and growth which are elements of productivity. In this sense, the concept applies universally. I hope you are also convinced of the importance of increasing the productivity of the work organization for the betterment of yourself and the entire world from an economic point of view.

Second, I hope this chapter will provide an overview of the factors and forces that influence productivity. Third, I would like you to gain a keener awareness of how people influence your organization's success. This refers to all people, but with a special emphasis on the members of your organization and why it is important for them to participate, to the extent practical, in the affairs of the organizaton.

Achieving these objectives will give you a new way to look at organizations which will be useful in making decisions about your role in them. I would like to ask that you proceed with a little more faith than skepticism at this point---faith in the concept that participative organizations are better for work organizations than less participative ones. Without this faith, you will be constantly evaluating the ideas presented in a negatively challenging mood and thereby denying yourself your own ideas that may be generated by reading with an open mind. Try to accept the ideas in this book as one observer's thoughts that can serve as a springboard for your own.

While one purpose of this chapter is to give you a fresh way to look at your organization, it should be stated that this new way is not the only way you should look at your organization, nor is it necessarily the best way. What is best very much depends on why you are looking at it in the first place. Just as you can look at a person and think of him/her as a statistic, a potential customer, a proud bearer of your family name, the provider, a sex object, or a target---and be right in any case, so can you look at your organization in many ways for different purposes.

If you are the typical business school graduate of the past thirty years and you wish to be objective about sizing up the needs of an organization, you will probably think in terms of five M's. Men, machines, money, materials, and markets. There is still some validity in this model. People are essential and always will be if we accept the definition of organization that I am using in this book, "Two or more persons interacting within a mutually recognized power relationship for some common purpose." Similarly, machines, if we interpret machines to mean technology, are a necessary part of the organization. Technology here refers to techniques as well as equipment, and encompasses everything from the largest machine in a production facility to a pencil. It also covers the procedures that members of an organization use to communicate with each other, plan their time, and do their work.

Money, or something that can readily be exchanged
for goods and services outside of the organization, is
undeniably necessary. I can imagine very small and very
temporary organizations being able to get along without
money or its equivalent, but these are the exceptions and
do not apply here. We are discussing the common
organizations of which we are all members: organizations
we use to earn our livings, educate ourselves, worship,
find social expression, or to meet our many and varied
needs.

Materials are the raw goods and services that our
organizations use to create new goods and services that
the customers or recipients of our organizational efforts
receive. Again, we could no doubt find exceptions, but
the vast majority of organizations need supplies and
suppliers even if they are such mundane items as taxi
rides, telephone calls, and stationery.

Markets would appear to be the most debatable of
the five M's. After all, only a small portion of all the
organizations in the world are commercial enterprises
that sell their wares or services to customers. But again,
we must think in broader terms. If an organization has a
reason for existing, and it must or it would automatically
disappear, it has a market in this sense. It does
something for someone in exchange for something else.
Let's take for example a poker playing group. People
organize themselves, using appropriate technology in the
form of cards, suitable furniture and game rules and not
only play with money, but use it to buy the cards and pay
for beverages, which are, incidentally, the materials they
need to make the organization work. Now what is the
market for the services of this organization? The
market, of course, is the players themselves. Yes, the
members of the organization can also be the clients.
More about this will follow.

You may be wondering, at this point, why I have
bothered to explain the validity of a model of organization needs that dates back to the early days of the
Industrial Revolution when I also said that I wanted to

give you a new way to look at your organization. If you are, please bear with me for a moment, and you'll understand. The five M approach can still be useful when planning a new organization or analyzing an existing one, but the trouble with the five M approach is the same as that with an old formula for executive functions. Business schools still teach that a leader's job is to plan, organize, lead and control. It's true these are important functions. However, they should be looked at as being quite limited and valued about as much as the old saying, "Build a better mouse trap and the world will beat a path to your door." The saying is a quaint reflection of the optimism of the Industrial Revolution when new technology was hungrily sought and envisioned as the cure for all ills of our species. This chapter is not about the money, machines, materials and markets covered by the five M model. You can find out about these from a great number of other sources. It also is not about the increasingly important environmental forces not covered by the five M model. I'm referring to the social and political pressures that can either aid the organization with various services and support systems, or strangle it with laws, regulations and informal demands that make existence a constant struggle.

This book isn't about the usual things leaders think about most when they create or lead an organization...it's about the things that specialists in organizational behavior think about. It's about what social and behavioral scientists, sociologists, industrial and social psychologists, and organization development practitioners think about when they study organizations. It's about people: men and women and their relationships to each other, their work and the organization. It's about the first of the five M's---by far the most important---in ways that are both new and sophisticated, and as old as common sense.

Ideally, when a specialist looks at an organization he/she should take in the entire picture, just as a doctor should have an understanding of a patient's medical history, home life, economic conditions, hereditary traits and other current environmental conditions. I know this sounds hopelessly idealistic and in fact, this rarely takes place. But remember, I said ideally. Similarly, an organization development specialist should be aware of all influences on the organization. In reality most of his/her time and efforts are centered on the members of the organization and their relationships. This is enough; people are at the heart of most organization problems and opportunities. If treated right, people, members of the organization, can help management deal with the other areas.

There are, of course, many examples of organizational problems that cannot be directly traced to the interaction of members of the organization. Loss of a major market, new government regulations, new technology, a natural disaster, or an economic depression could all ruin an organization and not be attributable to the talents, cooperation and motivations of the members of the organization. However, given minimal suitable external support conditions, adequate technology, sufficient finances, materials and markets, most problems are people problems. Similarly, most opportunities are people opportunities. You and the others in your organization affect it most. People working together can probably overcome the most adverse conditions. Conversely, non-integration or misintegration of individuals and groups can ruin an organization in the most favorable situation.

Unfortunately for us all, many leaders do not fully appreciate the potential value of capable people properly integrated and devoted to making the organization successful. They still think of people as raw materials or machines that if properly bought, oiled, and polished, will serve the needs of the organization. People, they reason, are plentiful and if they are compensated comparably to members of similar organizations will do their jobs or play their parts.

The best analogy to this type of thinking is the person who tries to solve all financial problems by making more money. They reason that, "So what if I make mistakes in purchases, or I'm careless about what I buy and how much I spend and what I spend it on. There is more where that came from." Self indulgence can feel luxurious and liberating to the person so fortunately endowed. It may elicit feelings of resentment on the part of those not so fortunate. But that is not the point of the analogy. Financial wastefulness is not as expensive, cruel, or wasteful as underutilizing people. I do not present this argument for humanitarian reasons; I make this argument on behalf of organization success. Misuse and mistreatment of people is enormously wasteful and our economy is finding it a difficult burden to bear.

As you know, this book is primarily about work organizations---the ones that most people serve to get the money they need to live. The productivity of such organizations in the West has steadily risen for many years, due mostly to advances in technology and the growing level of education and skill of the work force. We are currently experiencing a slowdown of productivity gains in the United States and other major western industrial nations. The growth curve is virtually flat. There is currently much talk about our need to become more like the Japanese in order to compete with their apparent capacity to constantly increase their industrial productivity. Personally, I don't believe the American culture will ever become like the Japanese culture. In fact, the Japanese culture is becoming more American. Visitors to Japan from the United States have long remarked on how Americanized the Japanese have become. They point to baseball, bikinis, pollution, cars, and electronic gadgetry. These are only superficial similarities. Much of Japanese technology was no doubt Western in origin, but the Japanese not only copied, they surpassed us in many fields of endeavor. They have been able to do this so well because of a long tradition of collectivist thinking that is in contrast to the individualism of the West. This is particularly true of the United States where many of our cultural values can be directly traced to the frontier and the great rewards it held for the competent, competitive, individualistic pioneer. The great diversity of our culture is not likely to evolve into a relatively homogeneous culture like that of the Japanese.

As mentioned, current indications are that individualism is on the rise in Japan. Studies conducted over a forty-year period among Japanese workers show a steady growth in the forces of "What's in it for me?" and a corresponding decline in the forces of "Will it contribute to harmony among us?" The latter is described by the Japanese as the Wa spirit. The Japanese practice called Ringi systematically involves all workers in major decisions---which incidentally causes slow decisions, but fast and efficient implementation. This is undoubtedly a factor in the high productivity level of their manufacturing organizations. We can learn much from this practice, but we must keep in mind that Wa the spirit, and Ringi the practice, have a long cultural tradition behind them and are constantly reinforced by everyday expressions of values. Traditionally, Japanese are hired for life, and are dismissed for only very extreme negative behaviors, whereas many American companies will lay off thousands during relatively minor economic downturns, mergers, or introductions of new technology that eliminate the need for certain workers.

To summarize, it seems that collectivism and productivity go hand in hand. It further seems that the individualism of the West is not likely to change and that its spread to the East will eventually erode productivity gains there.

If these assumptions are true, the only hope for increasing productivity in an organization, other than better technology and skills, is to increase the spirit of Wa and adopt practices such as Ringi. How can we do this when more and more of us sing "I did it my way"?

Napoleon said that he would let someone else write a country's laws if he could write the country's songs. By songs he meant not only songs, but also the proverbs, sayings, poems and other expressions of cultural values. He knew that it is values that govern behavior, not abstract laws written by either all-powerful rulers or the most democratically elected legislators. The support of the Wa spirit by cultural values is a more powerful influence on actual behavior than training in Ringi will ever be. Our conscious minds can tell us to curb our smoking or our eating, but years of habits reinforced by social norms are not easily denied. Attempts to instill the Wa spirit in our society and specific organizations are constantly being made. The appeal of living in situations where values are clear and commonly accepted is powerful to some. It is particularly attractive to confused, hurt, and other-directed individuals. Current news coverage would have us believe that religions requiring total devotion, and communal living experiments are on the increase. This would seem to indicate a trend toward collective thinking. The news coverage is out of proportion to the phenomenon. Antisocial and individualistic behavior are prevailing, for good or ill, depending on your values.

Does this mean we must either promote cultural values like traditional Japanese ones or be satisfied with less productivity? I don't believe these are our only alternatives.

Attempting to imitate traditional Japanese behavior is neither likely nor practical. Despite the efforts of cheerfully paternalistic corporate leaders and popular seminars in positive thinking, emotionally well adjusted people will not deny their training in critical thinking, nor should they if they are to solve the technical and social problems our organizations face.

We can find a compromise. Perhaps opposing traditions like "looking out for number one" and "doing or dying for old Siwash U" are forever incompatible. Perhaps we as a species will always divide into hero worship or team worship groups, but I believe there is hope for the objectivity camp. We can learn to know ourselves, others, and our organizations. We can teach people participative concepts, show them how to use them to both their own advantage and the organization's, and minimize the conflicts without hypocrisy. We can then continue to edge our productivity levels upward at a price we are willing to pay.

I hope you are the type of leader who can "buy into" this kind of value system because you will then learn to use the techniques offered with a minimum of internal anguish.

Some of you, no doubt, will find it a discomfort to give up the control techniques you now use. Achievement will move the individualist, and approval of authority the collectivist, but to appeal to the objectivist that resides in every one of us you will have to adopt new approaches.

I said earlier that your people are the key to your organization's success and that the extent that you are able to utilize them will be the measure of your success. Just to put this "people" business in perspective, let's look at all the constituent groups that have a stake in your organization. First, of course, are the members: you and the others who belong to the organization and who recognize that they do. This is the focus group and the one that this book is about, but for positioning, let's look at the other groups that have a stake in the organization. They are the owners of the organization; the clients, customers or users of the organization; and the people who make up the society in which the organizations operate, which includes a very important sub group---the suppliers. These three, plus the members, all have a say in organization matters either directly or indirectly. All want something from the organization and all are willing to give something to it.

The intriguing aspect of identifying the special interests is that the interests may be peopled by the same or by different persons. For example, a foreign subsidiary of a publicly held corporation is subject to the laws of the political entities governing the areas where it operates. The owners of its assets are the stockholders; it serves another group known as customers or clients, and is staffed by still another group known as the members or employees.

On the other hand, in a communal state, the same people are the encompassing society---the owners, the clients, and the members of the organization. On a smaller scale, a fraternal lodge, while part of a larger society, may be owned, dedicated to serving, and operated by the same individuals. Some charitable organizations are owned and staffed by the same people but dedicated to serving an entirely different group. And as a last example, a country club may be owned by the members, for the members' pleasure, but actually operated by a staff of paid employees. The latter would be the real members in the sense that I am using the term. Those who would normally be called the members are actually the owners and clients of the organization.

When you ask organization leaders which of the special interests---society, owners, clients, or members are most important to their organization, you will usually be answered with some variation of this statement: "They are all important because they are all interdependent." And the statement is, of course, true. However, if you should examine the policies and practices of those in authority within the organization, and the attitudes they reflect, you'll see that the organization tends to be either more society-oriented, more owner-oriented, more client-oriented, or more member-oriented. This tends to be true even when all interests are staffed by the same individuals. Leaders tend to measure their own success and the success of their organizations according to their basic orientation. Society-oriented leaders judge their efforts by the impact of the organization's activities on the physical and social environment. This could include the citizenry, the atmosphere, the social climate, or future generations. It also includes the reactions of society as manifested by the courts and regulatory agencies of the governments involved.

Leaders who are owner-oriented tend to evaluate success using such criteria as: return on investment, earnings per share, share of market, attainment of stated objectives, and performance comparisons with similar organizations.

Client-oriented leaders tend to evaluate the organization by the quality of service or goods produced as compared to previous years or to that offered by comparable organizations. They also consider the client's costs, whether it be in money, energy or convenience.

Member-oriented leaders naturally tend to judge the success of an organization by how well it meets the individual and collective needs of the members. While many of our human needs have been known for centuries, others have more recently come to light as a result of research in the behavioral sciences. These will be discussed in the next chapter.

Despite a leader's basic orientation, he/she will give at least lip service to the importance of considering the interests of the society, the owners, and the clients and members, whether they are separate individuals or groups or whether they are roles played by the same persons. Also, most leaders recognize that the needs of one interest group don't have to be met at the expense of the others. It is possible for all four to have their needs met, and this is probably the best measure of an organization's true success. It is the kind of organization that excels and the kind that most people feel best about owning, being served by, or being a member of.

At one time in the not too distant past, commercial organizations were simply not expected to consider the needs of society or their clients other than the extent to which they were directly related to meeting the owner's needs. Member needs were hardly considered at all. The industrial and commercial world has come a long way since the days of laissez faire capitalism. It also has come a long way since Henry Ford exclaimed, "All that we ask of the workers is that they do the work set before them."

At one time, Ford's remark may have been considered the epitome of modern and enlightened industrial organization policy. After all, he did lead the industrial world in raising worker income levels so they in turn could buy more of the fruits of their own labor. By doing so, he satisfied one member need, a basic human one: the need for income and the power to provide for the necessities of life. He probably did not realize that other needs abound in the psyche of modern man which may be just as compelling.

Modern leaders recognize now, more than ever before, that even the most extreme owner-oriented organization must consider the needs of its members as well as those of its clients and society at large. The most successful organizations now pay special attention to all four interests.

CHICAGO RESEARCH AND TRADING GROUP, LTD.
440 SOUTH LA SALLE STREET
CHICAGO, ILLINOIS 60605

CHAPTER 2

WHAT YOUR ORGANIZATION NEEDS
TO BECOME MAXIMALLY PRODUCTIVE

What your organization needs to achieve its greatest potential levels of productivity is the best possible use of its resources. Since the use of all resources is dependent on human activity, the use to which you put your human resources is the key to organization performance. If you have any experience at all at being a prince(ss)---a person with position power in an organization---you probably have already come to that conclusion and may be wondering why I have devoted a chapter to a concept that can clearly be stated in the first paragraph. The reason is that while the answer seems simple, in fact it is not. Learning how to use these marvelous human resources is what this book is all about.

Following are internal things an organization needs in addition to sufficient capital, adequate technology, materials, markets, and a reasonably supportive environment to achieve its full potential:

1. You---a participative prince(ss).

2. Competent people---members who care about the organization.

3. A mission---a clear and concise expression of organization purpose.

4. Goals and objectives for all members and units.

5. A design that suitably assigns functions and roles to individuals and units.

6. Structure that appropriately distributes power among the members of the organization.

7. A network or substructure that facilitates participative problem solving and project planning uncontaminated by the design and structure of the pyramid.

8. A communication system that efficiently gathers, stores, and distributes useful data.

9. A reward system that encourages your people to behave in productive ways.

10. A sufficiently powerful "Orgeist" or spirit of objective cooperation.

You

Allow me to expand a bit on each of these factors. First, you. Assuming you are the most powerful person in your organization or sub-unit, you must have a personal dedication to objective and subjective participation. This is an essential ingredient. If you choose to be participative from a rational, objective point of view, but your heart isn't in it, you will have to go through a painful period of adjustment. You will have to force yourself to do things that don't feel comfortable. This will take great intellectual confidence in their rightness.

If you already have the natural tendency to be participative, you'll have to examine your motivations. We'll talk more about your needs in Chapter Four so there will be no need to explain further here. But always keep in mind that you, or the most powerful persons in any organization are the sine qua non, the absolutely essential element to making participation work: the type of participation which leads to more effective usage of human resources, which in turn leads to achieving full organizational productivity. You must not only want to lead participatively both at the head and heart levels, but you must know how to do so.

Competent People

We also have a whole chapter devoted to people
and their needs, so there is no need to be too elaborate
here, but a few points should be mentioned now because
they too are absolutely essential to the high achieving
organization.

It is obviously sound advice to recruit competent
people who care about the success of the organization,
its performance, its mission, its goals and its ultimate
and continuing success. Is this difficult? Yes it is. Is
there any foolproof way to do this? No, there isn't.
Does this mean we shouldn't try? No, it emphatically
does not!

It is not my purpose here to give any advice on the
various selection and assessment devices and services
that abound in the marketplace for selecting salesmen,
technicians, managers, marriage or sex partners, or for
any other type of membership in any type of organization. Some are excellent and some are worse than
useless. You'll have to make that a separate investiga-
tion. Regardless of the personnel selection techniques
you use, remember that people have a way of changing
and so do organizations. This is particularly true in our
time and in our culture. Therefore, the extent that you
can expect to use a person's personality to predict
performance is highly limited, perhaps to only a few
months.

The method I suggest is an open discussion between
the prospective member and those members of the
organization to whom he/she will report and be in close
contact. This method is now widely used but rarely
within a framework of terms and procedures suitable for
expressing personal and organizational needs and relationships. To do this people must be given instruments
and data, plus the opportunity and encouragement to
explore their relationship needs. Trial-marriage type
arrangements can be used, assuming neither party is
risking more than they should, but trials are rarely like

the real thing. Finally, I suggest that the precedent of openly discussing specific relationships be established early and be reinforced with more discussions at periodic intervals. Inability to talk about relationship problems is the biggest obstacle to overcoming them. An instrument designed to facilitate discussion for prospective parties to a work relationship is one of the resources described in Chapter 11 of this book.

Mission

Successful organizations tend to have clear, widely understood statements of mission. More and more frequently you see organizations incorporating their statement of mission into their logos or major promotion pieces. The motto of the Chicago police department is "We serve and protect." More familiar slogan-mission statements include "Service is our business" and "People serving people." These are not only public relation slogans to impress society and customers, they are mission statements that give guidance to the members of the organization.

I would like to suggest that this need to define the organization mission be encouraged in all the sub-units within the organization. "We seek profitable new products," says R & D. "We sell at a profit," says marketing. "We produce clear, understandable reports," says data processing. Perhaps these mission statements seem too obvious to mention, but for most organizations and sub-units within large organizations, they are important to performance. Both individuals and organizations flounder when they lack a clear sense of purpose. Assuming that your people have a common understanding of their mission is dangerous. In case after case, my colleagues and I find wide disagreement among members over the mission of their organization.

Note that it is not enough for the leaders or owners to have a clear mission statement in mind for the organization. It must be shared and accepted widely by the members of the organization. It's true that it is easier to define the mission of some organizations than it is for others.   Those which have relatively simple functions and goals, such as athletic teams and production organizations are easiest. A higher percentage of members in such organizations will have common answers. Naturally there is a correlation between simplicity or clarity of mission and the ability to engender esprit de corps. This fact, you will see, can be a negative factor in some organizations.

Goals and Objectives

I tend to use the term goals for more distant targets such as those developed in long-range planning sessions. While these can be precisely stated, we know that time has a strange way of altering circumstances and the effort put into precision is often wasted.

Objectives are more immediate targets and can be more practically stated in quantitative terms. MBO or Management by Objectives systems adapted by many organizations integrate the objectives of each individual and unit with those of the entire organization. Testimonial literature abounds on the topic of MBO; however it must be emphasized that an MBO system that is perfect from a design point of view can lack the organizational spirit necessary to make it work as it should. When this is the case the system is less than useless and may even be detrimental to individual and organizational interest.

Organization Design

Another essential ingredient for the participative organization is commonly referred to as design and refers to the division of labor. Who is to perform what functions? Quite obvious you say. The concept probably goes back well beyond the great thinkers of antiquity. The most primitive tribes assigned roles for hunting and cooking, child care and leadership. Role assignments are that basic to human organization. Yet in our time, I would venture to say it would be difficult to find a more common cause of poor organization performance. Many such problems can be traced to people either not knowing what their role is or what the roles of other organization members are.

An exercise I often use in workshops or consulting sessions is to ask a manager and one of his subordinates to list the five or ten most important job responsibilities of the subordinate in order of their importance. Sometimes I also ask them to indicate the number of hours the subordinate should be spending on the various activities. As you probably have guessed, it is rare when the answers of the two people correlate to any great degree. This happens all the time, not just in small, new or unsophisticated organizations, but in some of the largest, richest and best equipped companies, agencies and social organizations in the world. This is true despite the fact that job descriptions and position responsibilities charts have been a part of organization technology for decades. It's true that organizations have managed to get by for years with poorly defined and poorly communicated member roles. However, to become optimally productive, members should be thoroughly familiar with their own roles and those with whom they interact most. They should have a general idea of the roles of those with whom they interact occasionally and be able to find out the roles of those with whom they may interact with on an occasional basis. The same statements made about people can be made about departments, units, or other divisions of the organization.

Power Structure

A logical, sensible distribution of power is still essential for the maximally productive organization. The day is coming when any sizeable organization wouldn't dream of vesting the bulk of power at the top of the pyramid. The reason is simply because organization specialists can show that people work better and more productively when power is distributed more evenly.

However, there will be struggles for power as long as there is power to be had. I prefer the definition that says: "Power is the ability to get your way!" There will be position power derived from rank in the organization. There will be expertise power, personality power, and power that results from control over certain resources. We are political animals, as Aristotle observed so long ago, and will always seek power to take care of "number one," or to do what we think is in the best interest of the organization.

There is nothing wrong with power. Certainly it can corrupt and the more absolute it is, the more certainly it will corrupt, as Lord Acton observed. But it can also get very worthwhile things done. Denying a person power may inhibit corruptive acts, but it can also inhibit worthwhile ones. There will always be times when a democratic or consensus approach is foolish, unnecessarily time consuming, or even dangerous. This can be so particularly when time or specialized knowledge are factors.

If we agree that power is necessary and accept that it is impractical and perhaps impossible to be evenly distributed at all times, we must accept the need to have a structure of power relationships for the organization. The much maligned organization chart is, and always will be useful if it honestly portrays power relationships.

An interesting and promising development in organization design technology is the so-called "matrix" organization. Large, complex, project oriented organizations such as giant construction companies have found it more cost effective to make various support units independent of line units and project leaders. This enables people and other resources to be assigned to the project leader that needs them most at any given time.

This means, for example, that the director of a dam construction project will not have complete control over the electrical engineering team. The top electrical engineer would report to both the project manager and the head of electrical engineering in the company. Note I did not say a "dotted line" or a "keep me informed" relationship. I said reports directly to both. Organizations that have these matrix relationships within the pyramid report that the design presents special problems and makes many management jobs difficult. They also report that matrix organizations are here to stay and will grow in number simply because they permit human and other resources to be used more efficiently. Those leaders who find matrix situations most difficult to manage are those who tend to be non-participative. Naturally participative managers and those trained to deal with split power relationships report that matrix situations pose no great problem.

Organizations with well established matrix cultures seem to have a lower incidence of interpersonal and intergroup conflict. It seems that the fluid structure promotes more, and shorter term relationships that are more collaborative in nature. It seems that organization design can influence the behavior of the members in very profound ways.

Network or Substructure

To overcome the communication blocks, rivalries and conflicts promoted by a pyramid structure, you need a substructure that promotes communication and problem solving without threatening the power structure. This requires every member who is considered a significant resource to the organization to belong to one or more permanent groups where his or her talent and knowledge can be channeled throughout the organization. The substructure links all such groups together in some practical way. Much more about this in Chapter Seven.

Communication System

All organizations need a system for gathering and distributing data in order to operate. Participative organizations need more. The more you expect people to solve problems and make decisions, the more information you can expect them to want and need. This applies not only to the hard or what I call formal information that comes in the form of reports, printouts, meetings or memos. It also applies to the soft or informal data that is part of everyday organization life.

There is no greater complaint in work organizations than that related to poor communications. What is usually meant is that there is a lack of sensitivity on the part of those in power about letting others in on what could be useful information for them to have. At times these complaints can be interpreted to be status complaints. That is, certain information in an organization is only given to those with rank and status---the "in" group. Not to get it is a sure sign you are not one of the elite. Hence the scramble to justify the need for information and the complaints when it is not forthcoming.

Participative organizations require greater sensitivity on everyone's part when it comes to information distribution. This is not only to placate sensitive egos, but more importantly to make sure that those who participate in decision making are sufficiently informed.

We will talk in more detail about the kind of information people need to function in participative organizations in the following chapter. Suffice it to say here that getting, storing, retrieving and using information is a primary function of all organizations and the maximally productive organization does it with order, precision, speed, and sensitivity.

Reward System

I prefer to classify rewards as either formal or informal. The formal rewards are any response to an organization member's behavior that he/she perceives as a response to that behavior---the key word in the sentence is "perceives." While you may be convinced that your compensation system is the finest anywhere, it will not encourage your people to behave in productive ways if they perceive their pay and other measurable rewards as unfair, inadequate or poorly administered.

The same holds true for "informal" rewards: all the organization responses experienced by the members that tend to encourage or discourage certain behavior. This includes many factors that are or can be interpreted in widely different ways by different individuals. I am speaking of such things as the nature of work assignments; relationships with leaders, peers and subordinates; confidence in leadership; security; and opportunities for various forms of growth.

Spirit

Orgeist, the spirit of objective cooperation, is the most essential ingredient that an organization must have to reach a state of maximum productivity. Not the traditional western (especially American) esprit de corps, nor the eastern Wa. It is a spirit, however, and I choose to call it "Orgeist." It is a term that I introduced in an article on Organization Development in the Encyclopedia of Professional Management published by McGraw Hill (1979). The term is a combination of org, which is short for organization, and geist, the German word for spirit. In my mind it fits with the terms philosophers are fond of using for the spirit of the times (Zeitgeist) and the spirit of the world (Weltgeist).

I chose to invent a new word rather than use esprit de corps or Wa because I believe these terms are too limiting. Esprit de corps connotes a heightened sense of unity and purpose shared by the members of an organization. Usually this spirit centers on some charismatic leader or holy cause. It can be a very powerful influence on behavior and it can stimulate groups or organizations

to excel and achieve remarkable victories and accomplishments. Those involved with organizations having a
high esprit de corps feel they have been led to exceed
their own expectations, to be part of something grand,
bigger than themselves. This phenomenon is most
apparent in athletic competitions when the team with
the greater esprit de corps beats an opponent that is
equal or greater in all other respects.

However it is possible for esprit de corps to work
against the best interests of the individual and the group.
Two military examples come to mind: Pickett's Charge
during the American Civil War and the Charge of the
Light Brigade during the Crimean War. In both cases
esprit de corps clouded judgment and fooled the attack-
ers into thinking that they could overcome superior
position and fire power. They suffered terrible defeats.
While the risks of esprit de corps in a work organization
are rarely as great as in war, and are usually greater
than in most athletic competitions, it is probably wiser
to promote cooperation through more objective measures.

From what I understand about the Japanese spirit
of Wa, the rallying point is not the leader, a symbol, or a
cause, but group harmony. It promotes thinking that will
go to great lengths to avoid directness and confrontation.
I believe the excesses of Wa find expression in hara-kiri
and kamikase practices, which obviously are as dangerous
as the excesses of esprit de corps.

The Orgeist is the spirit of objective cooperation,
of openmindedness, of risk taking, of trust, of freedom to
disagree with any group or person of any rank and power.
It connotes objectivity, confrontation without conflict,
sensitivity, respect for the individual and trust in his
concern for you, for the organization and its mission.
The Orgeist, like the esprit de corps, or Wa, can be weak
or strong and all can be highly positive. The big
difference is that you can have an organization with a
high Wa or esprit de corps, but one that supresses
individual expression. The Orgeist, however, promotes

unity, respect, and commitment to mission, but encourages free argumentation on policy, techniques, practices and strategy, and even of mission and goals. It also allows expression of "What's in it for me?" The spirit is an abstraction, but we know it is real. It both arises from the organization and flows back into it. It affects every person, every relationship and every activity.

The Orgeist is manifested and best observed in the form of norms. Norms are those unwritten rules of behavior that every group or organization has. Some are obvious such as dress habits: "We all wear ties and jackets once we make manager," and some are common greeting and parting rituals: "How's the boy?" "Hanging in there!" "Take care now!" "Have a nice day!" "You bet." Some are definitely counter productive: "Around here no one takes less than an hour and ten minutes for lunch." Or norms can be contributive to organization performance: "Everyone tries to bend over backward to get the orders out in an emergency," or "We always thrash out a problem and listen to everyone's point of view before making a major decision." Norms are the proof of a spirit---the Orgeist. More about norms later in the chapter about people needs.

I will end this chapter with a story that I like to believe is true. It is attributed to Sir Christopher Wren, the famous architect of 18th century London. It seems that Wren was making his rounds of several construction sites, and at each one he asked the workmen what they were doing. Typically he would get answers such as "We're earning our daily bread." Sometimes he would be told that the men were "Plying their trade." In a few places he was told that the men were digging a foundation or building a wall. But when he put his question to a group of stone masons on the construction site of Saint Paul's Cathedral, he was told by a spokesman, "If you'll let us get on with it, me and these other blokes will build the finest cathedral in all Christendom, guvnor." Wren beamed with delight and stepped aside to let the men continue their work.

The fact that Saint Paul's stands today as one of the great edifices of the world testifies that competent people worked within a suitable organization design and power structure and had the information they needed to do their work. But it is the story that tells us that a participative prince shared his mission with his people and helped them to care about it by infusing them with a strong <u>Orgeist</u>---the spirit of objective cooperation.

CHAPTER 3

WHAT YOUR PEOPLE NEED TO ACHIEVE
THEIR PRODUCTIVE POTENTIAL

Among the few things we can say with any certainty about our species is that we tend to have a fear of the unknown. It was true when we sat huddled in the cave and listened to the sounds of the night, and it's true now when we wonder about why we behave as we do. Actually, we have a great need to explain all phenomena, not just those that appear to be threatening. We used to give names and human characteristics to natural phenomena such as wind and rain and fire as though giving them names and personalities made them understandable and easier to cope with. Today some of us find comfort in knowing the scientific names of the same phenomena even though we don't understand them. Names somehow are reassuring. They put things in place, in order. They reduce confusion and promote a sense of stability, harmony, and integrity.

This practice of naming or explaining things in oversimplified terms can be harmful to ourselves and others if we are not careful. To illustrate this fact, I ask seminar participants to read a list of ethnic groups and human characteristics and then identify the ethnic group most commonly associated with the characteristics. Before doing so, I assure them that I understand that they are not, of course, prejudiced, but to give me the answers "most other, more prejudiced people" would likely give. The characteristics are:

        --- Drunkards---barroom brawlers

        --- Power hungry and domineering

        --- Hit men, organized criminals

        --- Lazy, responsibility-shirking

--- Cheap, overly thrifty

--- Money grubbing, greedy

--- Overly concerned with sex

--- Dumb, brutish

--- Bigoted, narrowminded

--- Aloof, class conscious, formal

--- Cold, unemotional and unfeeling

--- Falsely courteous, sneaky and back-
stabbing

American middle class groups have no trouble in
quickly coming to agreement on what "most other, more
prejudiced people" would say are the ethnic groups that
are most likely to be identified with these traits. By the
way, you'll note these traits are all negative. There are
relatively few widely-held positive ethnic prejudices.

All of our prejudices may not be so blatant as the
traditional ethnic ones listed above, but we all do have
some sort of prejudices. We have them for a great
variety of psychological and cultural reasons. But the
major reason seems to be that the average person has a
need to explain what people do just as he/she needs to
explain all phenomena. The easiest way to explain
human behavior in the minds of the masses is to explain
it in terms of ethnic groups. The absurdity of this type
of thinking is the basis for the jokes and plots of many
stories and T.V. shows in contemporary America. Ster-
eotypical thinking about groups can also be found in
many large organizations. Answer these questions
without pondering them: In the typical company what
group throws company money around and spends a lot of
time partying and playing golf? Which group is most
likely to be wined and dined and showered with presents?
Which group is overly concerned with the feelings of the

employees? Which group seems to think they are intellectually superior to others? Typically, sales people are identified with spending indiscriminately and partying; purchasing people with being entertained; personnel people with being overly concerned with employees' rights and benefits; technical experts, such as scientists, actuaries, and engineers as feeling intellectually superior to others.

You may have very few prejudices. You may have them under control which means that you recognize that you have them and make sure they don't influence your behavior. But you do have them. We all do. You acquired them when you were not analyzing things objectively. You were programmed by your life experiences to think and feel certain ways about certain people, places, things, and events. Any event that makes you think about them triggers certain thoughts, feelings, and behaviors.

It is sad, but probably very true. You have prejudices. You probably tend to classify people. You have ideas and feelings about them and your feelings regarding them tend to be two dimensional---either good or bad. You know your prejudices. They can get in the way of your making rational and objective decisions. To be objective you will have to learn to think of people as individuals, each with his/her own unique mixture of personality variables. You'll have to resist any easy way of categorizing people and making decisions based on such classifications.

A chapter about people and their needs could be thousands of pages long. We continue to be the most misunderstood and most interesting phenomenon on the planet and our times have seen an explosion of new information about what we are and why we behave as we do.   To narrow down my discussion of people to something manageable, I'll write about people and their needs in general and in organization settings more specifically.   Particularly, we'll be talking about the people who work for you if you are a prince(ss) of the pyramid in a hierarchical organization.

I will touch on some of the more common personal and interpersonal needs we all have and then zero in on what people need in an organization setting to be productive. I hope this chapter will encourage you to think about people and their importance to your organization in a special way, not in terms of their ethnic group or any other grouping that doesn't relate to productivity. I also hope this chapter will help you to become more aware of your own prejudices about people and encourage you to control them. Finally, I would like you to become more familiar with the more common needs that we all have, but with special emphasis on the needs we have as members of an organization if we are to achieve our productive potential. I think you can readily see why these objectives could be helpful to you in order to obtain maximum productivity from your organization. Obvious or not, here are the reasons: As a real-life person, even though you are a prince(ss) in your organization you must deal with people. You can't deal with your organization in the abstract if you are to be a participative prince(ss). You know that maximum productivity comes from participative organizations where all members use their full capabilities not only to do the routine work of the organization, but also to solve problems and seek and exploit opportunities. In order for this to happen, people's needs must be met. You should, therefore, become familar with the needs of people in general and the specific organization needs of the people you interact with on a regular basis.

Before getting into our discussion of people needs, let's talk a moment about manipulation. The most commonly held idea about motivating people is best illustrated by a donkey that is hitched to a cart with a carrot dangling from a string which is attached to a stick which is attached to the wagon. The donkey needs food, so when it sees the opportunity to fulfill its need, it moves toward the need fulfiller, and in so doing, pulls the cart to which it is harnessed. If the donkey needs further stimulus, the driver can swat its rump with a stick so the donkey is prompted to move away from the source of pain. This concept is more manipulation than motivation. I definitely advise against learning about the needs of people just so you can use the needs as carrots. The reason is that, while you may get your organization cart moving through manipulation, it won't move as fast, as well, or as consistently as it would if your people were not being manipulated by the necessities of life in a cold, callous manner that implies you think of them as donkeys. I suggest that if you use a carrot and stick approach, make sure your people participate in determining what the carrot and stick will be and when and how long they should be used.

Personal Needs

Certain facts seem to apply to most humans most of the time. I make even this cautious statement with trepidation because our marvelous species seems so remarkably capable of doing the new and unexpected. Every time we feel we can confidently make generalizations about people, some person or group pops up and does something to make us look foolish.

Earlier I mentioned that people seem to have a fear of the unknown so they will invent explanations for phenomena they don't understand. I also mentioned that people seem programmed to want to preserve their own lives. This line of generalizations supports the pleasure/-pain concept which states that humans and all living things will tend to avoid pain and seek pleasure. All behaviors can, for all practical purposes, be traced to this basic program.

The pleasure/pain syndrome is more complex than it appears at first. What is perceived as pleasure or pain may differ from one person to the next. For some people the pain of failure or disgrace is as painful as death. For others the pleasure of a cigar is unmitigated by the fact that the smoke is painful and harmful to his/her lungs. It's true that we can identify many things that are almost universally considered as pleasure giving or pain giving, such as fresh air, water or fire. But other factors vary in

amount, intensity, location, timing, and so forth and
therefore provide many exceptions. It is dangerous to
generalize about what a particular person needs unless
we are prepared to recognize the possibility of exceptions popping up at any moment.

The fact that human beings have many needs and
that these needs vary from person to person and from
time to time, is partly explained by the conscious/sub-
conscious model of the mind. The conscious portion of
our brain supposedly deals with our rational thoughts and
allows us to be aware of them. The subconscious part
deals with feelings, behaviors and body functions that we
are unaware of and does so while we are awake or asleep.
It never stops functioning while we live. The conscious is
turned off during daydreaming, meditation, and hypnosis
as well as sleep. A more refined interpretation of this
concept suggests that we not think of the mind in two
separate categories, but as a gradual continuum from
highly alert consciousness to deep subconscious.

The discovery that the different sections of the
brain each control or at least largely influence distinct
mental functions is exciting. I have no doubt that future
research will uncover more specific correlations but
currently the idea of lobal functionality holds sway. The
right lobe not only controls the motor functions of the
left side of the body, it also seems to control our
intuitive and creative thoughts. It allows us to assimilate a great mass of information and stimuli and make
decisions about what is happening, should be happening or
could be happening. There is evidence that there is a
much higher degree of creativity among those who are
lefthanded.

The left side of the brain not only controls the
motor functions of the right side of the body, it is also
the center for systematic thought, for logical, sequential
thinking. It is the part that seems to let us analyze,
assimilate, quantify, and come to logical conclusions. It
appears to me more like the conscious part of our minds
and the right lobe sounds like the seat of the more
subconscious part of our minds.

Obviously, both of our lobes are highly important to our full development and many things from genetics and body chemistry to cultural conditioning can influence how and how much we tend to use the various parts of our mind. Professional people watchers say they can identify people who are predominantly right brained and those who are more left-brained controlled and those who seem to be influenced about equally by both lobes.

To transfer this information about brain functions to our model of human behavior based on needs, we can say that some people need to behave more intuitively and some more analytically and some to behave in both ways. The intuitive types feel it is pleasurable to cut through or ignore a mass of information and solve problems or at least make decisions with snap judgments. They prefer to avoid the pain of systematically sifting through the data their minds perceive through their senses. On the other hand, the analytical types seek the pleasure of sequential thinking and avoid the pain of ignoring what they perceive as they make their decisions about how to feel or behave.

Now, let's get down to some more specific needs. To see how they all fit together and to enable us to deal with this information, we are going to need some useful categories. Then with the categories and the specific needs you will have a checklist that you can use to observe and consider an individual's behavior and the needs he/she is trying to meet. The categories I find most useful are personal, interpersonal, and organizational. I will treat the first two briefly because the subject of this book in general and this chapter in particular is increasing productivity by meeting the needs of the people in organizational settings.

Certain personal needs can be also described as natural needs because they can most easily be related to the pleasure/pain program that nearly all of us carry around in our heads. They are statistically normal. Most people most of the time have certain common ideas about pain and pleasure. We feel the need to avoid damage to our bodies---burns, bruises, smashes, falls, bumps, etc. We also like to avoid too much noise, light, dampness, cold and heat. We have physical, mental and emotional needs that are natural to most of us.

Other personal needs have cultural foundations. We acquire them by living in a particular social melieu. Prior to our times with rapid transportation and communications and the migration of large numbers of people, the needs of individual members of a specific culture could be accurately identified. This is the origin of the ethnic stereotypes we talked about earlier. Perhaps the social style common to the villages of 19th century Ireland seemed alien when transported to New England. It appeared to normative New Englanders that all Irish were drunkards and barroom brawlers. But if there was ever a legitimate reason for assuming people of the same ethnic group had basically the same needs, it can hardly be used as an accurate predictor of behavior today. Cultural needs can be powerful. They can overcome natural needs designed to protect our lives. Members of primitive tribes as well as some modern peoples will mutilate their bodies with tattoos, holes and other disfigurement in the name of beauty, passage to adulthood, or religious devotion. Knowing a person's culture can give you some clues to his/her values or needs and therefore his/her behavior. But in the modern Western world it would be foolhardy to use traditional ethnic identification as anything more than a weak predictor of behavior.

Cultural groupings that are somewhat more reliable and can give clues to values, and therefore behavior include location of birth; area where growth during formative years took place; present residence; social class; educational level; and employment sector such as government, health care, educational institutions, military or industry.

Male and female cultural roles are becoming less distinct and may break down the sexual basis for determining values and roles. Age can be used as a behavioral determinant as can membership in certain demanding religious or political groups. But all of these determinants are relatively uninfluential by the standards of former times when people were restricted to a small geographical area and tended to be culturally homogeneous.

A third subcategory of personal needs is highly individual. These needs result from any unique combination of hereditary characteristics plus our life experiences. These particularly powerful needs are sometimes called "dominant motivators." Even these, however, vary in intensity from situation to situation and from time to time. Some of us have two or three or more dominant needs and some of us seem to have none at all.

One of the most common dominant motivators is the need to achieve and accomplish. This need is more prevalent in certain societies than others. It is the kind of need that employers like to see in employees because they assume the high achiever will want to achieve the organization's goals. Some people have a stronger need to win in competitive situations. Even if the situation isn't normally considered a competitive one, they will make it so. Others have a great need to be among friends. Still others have a drive to put structure and order in their lives and avoid ambiguous situations where everything cannot be safely categorized. Other fairly common dominant needs include: the need for security, the need for approval from authority figures and peer groups, the need to be esthetically pleased, the need to pursue altruistic causes, and the need to be of direct help to other individuals.

In general, people given the opportunity will seek roles, positions, and jobs that will tend to meet their dominant needs. But keep in mind that some people are highly flexible and can grow or change throughout their lives. Most students of the subject insist that need patterns are established early in life and stay the same throughout life. I, however, suspect that people can and do change and your perceptions of them can change as well. It really doesn't matter for practical purposes what has really changed. Just remember to make all of your judgments about people tentative and be receptive to signals that indicate you are typecasting and may be wrong.

Interpersonal Needs

This category of needs covers our relationships with other people in one-to-one situations and in some cases applies to group situations. There is, of course, a great number of possible relationships we might have with other individuals and all have a certain flavor to them. For example, husband/wife, doctor/patient, buyer/seller, father/son, mother/daughter, and so on. These, and probably all others, can be also discussed in terms of power, in terms of who has the greatest ability to get their way within the relationship.

The power aspect, like other things in a relationship, is a matter of perception. To paraphrase the famous saying about beauty, "Power is in the eye of the beholder." If you view someone as a power superior, inferior, or equal, it tends to affect your needs regarding that person. These interpersonal needs tend to vary with each individual you interact with. You could, for example, feel that you are more dominant when you interrelate with a specific person, which means that you intuitively feel that the other person expects you to lead the interaction and make any decisions regarding your relationship. Depending on your personal needs and how you feel about the other person, you might be either protective or exploitive of them. You might feel, "Here is someone I should nurture, help and protect." On the other hand, you might feel, "Here is someone I can use for my own purposes because he/she has given me the power to do so. "

A reverse situation would be one where you perceive another person to be more powerful. Here, too, you have a choice, although it will most likely be subconsciously made to be either compliant or rebellious just as children have forever been with parent figures. You may want to receive the approval of the dominant figure or you may feel that it is necessary to constantly rebel either overtly or covertly against this person you see as being stronger and more powerful than yourself.

A third set of interpersonal needs can be found in a relationship that you perceive to be one of peers or siblings. Such relationships tend to be more volatile than others and the feelings associated with them more intense. You may perceive the other person as one with whom you feel the need to cooperate because you share some common identification, cause, or enemy. On the other hand, you may feel the need to compete, to be on constant guard against, to seek ways to demonstrate superiority.

Of course, it is possible to be above all interpersonal needs as I have described them. You can interact with other people in a completely objective way and have no preconceived view of the relationship, hence not need to act any one way in particular. This would be an ideal situation where you must work together to solve problems. It would be like combining two computers to more than double the power of either one. It would be ideal but it wouldn't be human. We can expect it to happen naturally in only small percentages of our interactions.

We can, however, be aware that we all have interpersonal needs and that they affect our behavior and that they, like other needs, are linked to our pleasure/-pain value system that gives us a feeling of rightness or wrongness, of goodness and badness. Being aware of them and being able to identify them allows us to talk about them in an open way so they can be dealt with as part of the total problem-solving effort.

The Organization Needs of People

Now we come to those needs that people have as members of an organization. You'll find that the subcategories under this heading are similar to those offered in Chapter 2 where I covered what organizations need to become maximally productive. This is understandable. Organizations are people. The perspective of the individual is needed to understand how the success of the organization is dependent on individuals.

I have found a formula to be particularly useful in explaining to leaders how the many factors in an organization influence the behavior of its members. The formula is: $S \times C \times T \times M = I/O\ P$. The letters stand for: Structure, Communications, Training, and Motivation. The I/O P stands for Individual and/or Organization Performance or Productivity. I use the formula to emphasize the interdependence of the elements. Let's say we can assign a value of zero to ten to each variable on the left side of the formula. A value of ten for each would produce 10,000. Should, however, one variable be zero, the Performance will be zero even if all the others had a value of ten. Let's say an organization member had all the structure he/she needed to do his/her job, and the best possible communications, and he/she knew how to do his/her job, but did not want to do it. The formula would look like this:

$$10 \times 10 \times 10 \times 0 = 0$$

This formula helps those who think most performance problems can be solved by a training program to understand that other variables may be the real cause of poor performance. In a later chapter you will see how this formula can be used as a basis for diagnosing an organization. In this chapter I will tell you about the factors in the catagories used in our formula.

Structure

The category of structure refers to anything in the organization that officially influences the behavior of its members. It is a very important variable and it encompasses many elements. Here is a thumbnail description of the most common ones.

Design: People tend to work more effectively in social situations that they understand. In work environments this means a sense of relationship of the parts to the whole. They like to know what department does what, and who is assigned where. It gives them a feeling of cohesiveness, order and integrity.

Assignment: People need to feel that their particular set of duties relates to the overall design. It helps to have a clearer picture of how all the parts, including theirs, fit into the whole.

Power Distribution: People like to understand the exact pecking order: to whom they must be submissive and with whom they may be dominant, and with whom they are on an equal par. No one such structure is necessarily the best as long as whatever is in operation is understood and accepted.

Facilities: People need things like buildings, parking lots, lights and other environmental factors. They can be an influence on how people behave and how they feel about their role.

Equipment: This category covers the devices a person uses in the execution of his assignments, and can range from a helicopter to a pencil sharpener.

Supplies: People need raw materials and expendables that are used in the performance of their role assignments such as typewriter ribbons, dictation tapes, stationery, lumber, steel---whatever is used and possibly re-ordered on a fairly regular basis.

Technical support: This refers to the services
provided by other organizational departments or
members, or possibly outside services for purposes
of helping members of organizations do their jobs.
It covers all the traditional staff functions performed for the traditional line departments, but it
also covers all other dependencies as well---
janitorial services, research, word processing, pur-
chasing---anything done by one person or department to help other organization members do their
jobs.

Management Support: This term is used here and
refers to the permission that those with power give
to those with lesser power to do their jobs. While
power may be implied in the responsibilities assigned to an individual, the complexities of modern
organization life and the non-routine nature of
many jobs can make this particular variable an
extremely important one in terms of allowing and
encouraging individuals to put forth their maximum
effort.

Communication

Communication is the next element in our performance formula and generally covers the flow of information that people need to perform.   Here are the more
common elements in this category.

Technical data: This is any information that a
person needs to perform his/her role such as
blueprints, orders, catalogs, printouts, memos, letters, calls, and messages.

Operating rules and procedures: These are very
similar to technical data, but apply to the more
general organizational data as opposed to a specific
job or project.   How you apply for insurance or a
promotion, or how supplies are to be requisitioned,
and such, fit into this category.

Organization mission, goals, and strategies: These are the "big picture" items that people need in varying degrees to help them understand their relationship to the entire organization. Those who identify with their organization, even if they are at the lowest power levels, like to know what is going on.

Function and role assignments: People have a need to know what the individuals and departments with whom they interact are responsible for. While few members of a large organization want or must know what all others do to contribute to the organization success, almost all have the need to know what those close to them do and are responsible for.

Position responsibilities: These are the things a person is supposed to do to meet his/her membership obligations. It seems obvious that a member would have this need, but relatively few organizations provide this information in a clear, concise way.

Personal goals: These are largely a matter of assigning numbers to responsibilities: how much, by when, or in what time frame. Having specific goals is a proven way of promoting achievement and progress. Yet the practice of consistently having all members of the organization set and seek to attain specific goals is not very widespread. People need goals that mesh with the organization goals to be fully productive.

Performance feedback: This is a report on how a person is actually doing in relation to what is expected of him/her in the eyes of both peers and the powerful. This is usually limited to letting him/her keep their jobs. Most of us would prefer to know how others view our efforts so we can opt to change our behavior or correct misinterpretations of what we have done. Most people in most work situations do not receive adequate feedback to meet their needs.

Current events: This is a communication need that is not usually met by the grapevine. People have a real need to be informed of organizational happenings. They can then sift and use the data as they see the need. While the danger of inundating people with trivial information is real, the complete insensitivity to this need causes ill feelings and prevents technical data from reaching those who can use it.

Training

Training is the "how to" part of any organizational role. It is the part of our formula that is usually blamed for poor performance and productivity, but it is usually not the real cause. Nonetheless, it is a very important variable. A person cannot be expected to perform well if he/she simply does not know how to perform. Here are the major subheads we use to distinguish between the various types of training.

Job or technical skills training: Skills are used in the performance of a specific job as described in the position responsibilities chart or job description. The category can cover conducting a board meeting, adjusting a microscope, flying a jet, or balancing an account.

Self management skills: These skills are more universal in application, but still refer to what an individual does to play his role in the organization. Included in this category would be such skills as reading, writing, listening, speaking, time and activity planning, remembering, dictating, project planning, creating ideas, and problem solving. These are more or less universal skills that unfortunately, most people are assumed to possess just by growing up and participating in normal educational activities. Most adults and their organizations would benefit by refresher training in these areas.

Organizational membership skills: These refer to knowing how to operate within a specific organizational setting. They can be quite precise, such as how to file a grievance, or put in for a transfer, or fire a subordinate. The category also covers "unofficial" skills that deal with how to look good to powerful people, how to get your budget approved, or how to make the most out of the local social/political situation.

Interpersonal skills: These skills are used in dealing with other individuals of any power relationship and level of personal abilities for purposes of helping yourself and the organization. This is the area of training that is currently receiving the most widespread attention because of a belated recognition of its importance and because the state of the art is developing to the point where such skills can be taught effectively.

Consultative skills: These skills are closely allied to interpersonal skills. A growing awareness of the importance and interdependencies of all individuals and departments in an organization has heightened interest in the consultative role. Members of the organization with special skills and resources can often better serve other members by taking an objective problem solving stance, rather than providing a requested service. People in purchasing, data processing, and training, for example, need consultative skills to deal most effectively with both organizational peers and those more powerful than themselves in the organization.

Management skills: These skills help subordinates do their jobs or play their roles most effectively. Specific skills in this category include recruiting, hiring, training, counseling, coaching, directing, delegating, evaluating, and motivating others.

Motivation

The last major category in our performance formula is motivation or the "reward system" of the
organization. As you know at this point, motivation is
not something that can be thought of or treated as a
separate phenomenon because it is intertwined with all
the other elements of structure, communication, and
training, plus many personal and cultural influences from
outside the organization. There are, however, ways to
look at those things in the organization culture that tend
to prompt certain behaviors among the membership.
They can be divided into formal and informal and are
explained below.

FORMAL REWARDS

Formal rewards are things the organization intentionally does to encourage members to play their roles
well. Formal rewards are such things as salaries,
commissions, bonuses, profit shares, stock ownership
plans and other financial devices. The category also
includes non-monetary rewards such as promotions,
office location and decor, access privileges to organization resources, and various other status symbols. People
have the need to feel their organization's formal reward
system is as good or better than what they could have
elsewhere, and that it is fairly administered.

INFORMAL REWARDS

Informal rewards are "responses" in the organization culture that influence the behavior of the members,
but probably were not intentionally designed to do so.
They prompt people to help the organization reach its
goals and accomplish its mission. Following are the more
common ones.

Physical environmental conditions: This includes
everything from the colors of the walls to the
temperature of the water in the washrooms. Our
surroundings do influence how we feel, think and
behave. They obviously can influence the quality

and quantity of our work and our performance as organization members. This category seems like a duplication of the facilities category under the Structure heading, but is meant to emphasize esthetic qualities of the work place rather than the functional.

Nature of the work assignment: The activities people are required to do influence their behavior. While highly dependent on the perception of the individual doing it, challenging work is a rewarding experience.

Security, stability and predictability: These are widely recognized as human needs and most modern major organizations attempt to meet them for their members. While meeting them is not necessarily a stimulus to better performance, not meeting them is a decided detriment to performance.

Organization pride: This is identification with a group known for something the individual takes pride in. It can influence the individual to play his/her role in a way that will enhance the image of both self and the organization.

Confidence in the leadership: This is closely related to the pride one has in the organization. Pride is particularly important to complex organizations where few individuals have a clear understanding of how all parts fit together and how the organization relates to the world and the challenges it faces. This confidence also comes down to a personal level where the leaders demonstrate a sensitivity to the needs of the individual members, particularly their need for respect and information. Should the members feel they are mere pawns to be used for the personal glory of the leaders, you can expect objective cooperation to suffer.

Leader/follower relationships: These are between individual members and their immediate superior.

This relationship is vitally important to both morale and productivity and is fully explained in my earlier book, People, Power and Organization (AMACOM, 1973). The mismatch of styles between a leader and follower must be dealt with to maximize the performance of both parties.

Interpersonal and intragroup relationships: This refers to the interaction with individuals that an organization member comes into contact with most often in the course of playing his/her organizational role. These relationships can encourage or discourage productive behaviors. Group norms, the unwritten rules that govern so much of our behavior, are very influential in these interactions.

Intergroup relationships: These may be between formal or informal groups in the organization. Groups can be different departments, shifts, or ranks. They can also be unofficial groups based on race, ethnic background, sex, age, work location, politics, income, union status, etc. Should relations between groups be less than cooperative and supportive, the organization must suffer. To be maximally productive, individuals must not only feel good about their own group, but also relate well with the other formal and informal groups in the organization, particularly those with whom they must interact on a regular basis. All of the needs described above are related and should be considered separately only for purposes of trying to understand that which is both abstract and dynamic. Breaking out the elements and thinking about them individually gives us a way to systematically examine and intervene in the organization culture. We know that the more we successfully meet the needs of organization members, the more likely that the organization will be successful.

Perception

There is one major point that absolutely cannot be overemphasized when it comes to talking about what people need to achieve their productive potential. The point is this: all the needs mentioned above are not absolute. They are good or bad, met or not met, motivators or demotivators, depending on how the individual perceives them. You can believe and perhaps prove to your own satisfaction that the individual has all the structure, communication, training and motivation needed to play their role, but if the individual does not perceive it to be so, it is not so.

When you analyze or diagnose your organization or any of the individual members of it keep in mind that you are dealing simultaneously with your own perceptions and those of others. A true participative prince(ss) meets the needs of the organization and the needs of the members as THEY perceive them.

To provide transition to the next chapter, consider one final need your people have. They need to perceive you as valuing and encouraging their participative behaviors. You need, among other things, to have them perceive you as being participative. What you will require to be so perceived is covered in the next chapter. How you promote participation is covered in subsequent chapters.

CHAPTER 4

WHAT YOU NEED TO LEAD PARTICIPATIVELY

Everything you think, feel, and do at any given moment is the result of your inherited makeup, what you have experienced in the past, are experiencing at the moment, and anticipate happening in the future. Like everyone else, you are programmed to seek pleasure and avoid pain as you uniquely interpret these feelings and events. Like everyone else, your experiences have shaped your needs to seek pleasure and avoid pain in a unique way. Like everyone else, your behavior is expressed in patterns or styles. Like everyone else, you have the power to examine your own mind, to know yourself and to change not only your behavior and your style, but also your feelings, your values and your beliefs. It is important that you believe this.

It is axiomatic that we judge others by their actions and we judge ourselves by our intentions. It is important for you to understand how you perceive yourself and how others perceive you and how these perceptions affect your relationships and behavior. It is important because you are part and parcel of your organization, and as such what you do affects the system just as what the system does affects you. The more powerful you are, the truer this is.

Powerful leaders commonly tell their consultants by their behaviors if not their words that they wish to train and develop their people, not themselves. They seem to feel that men and women can be changed to make them behave more like the leader wants them to behave without the leader changing his/her own behavior. This is a hopeless assignment. There is no way to reap the benefits of participative management without management participation. This means in thought, word and deed. Unfortunately few of the high achievers who work themselves to the top of an organization are naturally programmed to lead participatively. If they were, there would be no need for this book, for consultants, or the entire management training and organization development establishment. Fortunately, people and organizations can change, and the healthiest, if not the easiest way to change, is through an individual and collective conscious willingness to do so.

Chris Argyris, writing in the 1977 March-April issue of the Harvard Business Review, reports on his extensive research into the behavior of CEO's---Chief Executive Officers---and their influence on organization behavior. He finds that CEO's tend to be all the things we in our culture expect leaders to be---competitive, articulate, persuasive. They are the winners in our culture. They believe in setting observable goals and achieving them. They admire these traits in others and claim they want their own subordinates to develop them. However, the CEO's behavior and attitude encourages conforming, boss approving, boat stabilizing behaviors.

This is the basic dilemma of organization life in our culture and perhaps most others: How can we get open, risk taking, respectfully confrontive, adult cooperation among leaders, followers and peers when win/lose competitiveness is the behavior that is rewarded from the cradle to the grave? This problem is greatly enlarged when it involves the very top person in a large organization, particularly a business organization. Ironically, these are the organizations that value and support participative management practices the most. The king of the hill becoming a member of the round table is a problem that is evident at the lowest levels of management as well as the top. So, whether your princely duties require you to sit high or low on the organization pyramid, you will have to cope with competitive attitudes and behaviors.

The general strategy I suggest is this: first have faith that the problem is solvable and then involve everyone concerned in seeking a solution. Don't become discouraged if the problem is never completely solved because there are great benefits to be gained by partially solving it and in the act of trying to solve it.

The biggest obstacle you face in becoming a participative prince(ss) is yourself. If you are a powerful person, it is probably because you sought the power either consciously or subconsciously. You sought power because you have a need for it. You have a need for it because it has a positive value to you. The social biologists may someday prove that the value you place on power is inborn or inherited, but I believe it came from your chosen role models and was reinforced by your life experiences. Having power is relatively pleasurable to you and not having it is relatively painful for you.

If you have already achieved considerable position power in a sizable organization, you probably not only have a need for it, you also have the skills for it. Your skills enable you to quickly, almost intuitively "read" a person, determine what gives them pain or pleasure, communicate to them that you can provide either one and that you will do so depending on whether or not they behave as you wish them to behave. This may be done overtly with raging or threats, or subtly with looks and gestures. Some call it manipulative or coercive or just Machiavellian. Some call it persuasiveness or leadership or just being political. Whatever it is called, those who practice it well are much admired and emulated. They can even become folk heroes like Howard Hughes or Chicago's late mayor, Richard J. Daley.

With these thoughts in mind, let us get on to some specific areas of what you require to become a participative prince(ss). There are five requirements:

1.   The power and opportunity to be participative.

2.   An understanding of what organizations, people, and you need to be productive, and how these needs interrelate.

3.   Skills, techniques, and procedures that encourage participativeness.

4.   Courage to overcome resistance from within and without.

5.   Judgment regarding when to lead, when to follow, and when to collaborate.

Requirement #1- The power and opportunity to be participive.

The prime element for leading participatively is power---position power in your organization. You have to possess it and your followers must perceive you as having it. Should you be a lame-duck leader or one in title only without the ability to deliver pleasure or pain, or if the situation is unstable politically, your people will be more concerned with keeping their own power or gaining more. They will not contribute to the Orgeist--- the spirit of objective cooperation. Paradoxical as it may seem, it is necessary to have control before you can share it. It is usually more difficult to start a participative enterprise or undertaking when the participants are peers. Such situations often lack the stability necessary for the rational exchange of information and ideas and the subsequent problem solving and planning that must take place. Of course there are many exceptions to this rule and as the educational level rises and participation skills proliferate, the phenomenon may not be so rare in the future.

CALM

Power alone is not enough. You also need the opportunity to be participative. One element of opportunity is relative calmness---lack of crisis. Fires in the waste basket always take precedent over delivery schedules, budget meetings, and long-range planning. Real, imagined or fabricated emergencies inhibit conjecture, discussion and planning and promote action regardless of how precipitous or ill timed. A crisis is the time for leaders to show their stuff and to be reaffirmed as the leader. A crisis calls for speedy decisive action. There is no time for extensive deliberation. If the organization is one that is consistently in a state of crisis to the extent that a combat platoon might find itself in time of war or a fire fighting unit in the midst of a natural disaster, then participation and participative leadership is clearly uncalled for. But for most organizations, real crises are rare. This is as it should be and if it is not, one can legitimately suspect that events are perceived and labeled as crises because it suits the needs of those perceiving them as such.

STRUCTURE

Another element of opportunity is the relative structure of the organization---the extent that the duties or functions performed by the members are routine or not self determined. Very flat organization charts are not conducive to participative management. One overseer can supervise one hundred coolies all doing the same things: one principal, many teachers. One insurance company I know of sells through the mail and has highly mechanized the roles of members of large departments. They hire people who understand the nature of the work and who like it. To promote participation in such a situation would be a disservice to the people and the economics of the situation. To some it would seem that the people are being used as robots or machines or computers and, in truth, they are. But who can argue with success, productivity, good feelings, and profits?

Please note that I am not saying such organizations should be led participatively to become maximally productive, but that certain units within the organization may perform adequately without a great deal of participation. It is possible to introduce elements of participation in even highly structured organization units. But in such cases, the interventions would not be of the team building or group development variety as described in

Chapter 7, but more of the participative behavior modification type described also in Chapter 7. This is where the people doing the routine tasks participate in determining what reactions from the organization will tend to encourage them to produce more, and more effectively.

Requirement #2- An understanding of what organizations, people, and you need to be productive, and how these needs interrelate.

In previous chapters I talked about what organizations need and what people need in organization settings to perform productively, so there is no need to elaborate on these subjects in this chapter. Since you are a "people" you naturally have the same needs, but as a person with power and a leader in the organization, your personal needs are somewhat different, at least in degree.

Primarily, you need to be perceived as a leader whose style is one of supporting responsible participativeness. Leadership style is one of those overworked concepts that means so much or so little depending on who you are talking to. Some writers treat styles in a non-model way. That is, they don't try to talk about categories or scales or types, but treat each person individually as some psychologists describe their patients. This seems like an honest and objective way to deal with individuals, but few leaders have the time, skills, or the background to so analyze people, even important ones like their own leaders or their immediate followers in the organization. Other writers on the subject lump all sorts of behaviors and characteristics into categories and try to pigeonhole leaders into them. These systems are suspect because of the lack of scientific data to prove that a given variety of behaviors tend to group together. This is often what is called armchair psychology and while fascinating to contemplate, is mostly invalid.

Other writers more legitimately reduce styles to one or two variables such as concern for follower and concern for task or being thing-oriented and people-oriented, or being democratic and autocratic. Most of these thinkers on the subject will be quick to point out that no one style is appropriate all the time. In general I concur with this view. My own method of dealing with leadership styles is fully explained in <u>People, Power and Organization.</u> It uses a straight-line continuum that represents the extent a leader tends to impose structure on his followers. I strive also to make the point that one position on the continuum is not any more desirable than another except in how it relates to the followers and the job situation. I also suggest that terms like autocratic or democratic be avoided because they connote value. I also make it a point to say that no one is at any one position on the style scale in any objective sense. They are there at any given moment only in the eyes of the beholder. What seems like high structure-imposing in the eyes of one follower may seem relatively permissive in the eyes of another or in one's own view.

The idea of determining style based on the extent a leader tends to impose structure has been widely accepted. It is logical, easy to understand, and useful for discussing relationships in a non-threatening way. It is also a backed up by research that proves followers tend to have higher morale when working for leaders whose styles match their own. Similarly, leaders tend to evaluate the performance of followers higher if they perceive their styles to match. I firmly believe the structure basis is the best, most useful way to talk about leadership styles. However, there are other behaviors and other styles a person may have. Understanding how they are perceived could contribute to better self understanding and the understanding of others.

Keep in mind that styles are characteristic ways in which we tend to meet our needs and should not be confused with moods that are more temporary in nature. While we have many needs in common, their relative strength and the way we attempt to meet them are apt to be extremely varied. Consider the following list of needs in order to make judgments about your own style of meeting them. The process may help you to know yourself better, which really is what this chapter is about.

PEER RELATIONSHIPS

How do you tend to deal with your siblings or peers? Are you more competitive or more cooperative or do you shift from one to the other? How do you feel about it?

PROBLEM SOLVING

How do you usually solve problems, particularly in your work? Do you tend to make decisions intuitively or do you carefully analyze all angles? If you are a switch hitter, when do you switch? Do you have any strong feelings associated with your style?

INTERPERSONAL COMMUNICATIONS

How do you tend to exchange information with others? Do you find yourself listening more or talking more? Are you a sender or a receiver? You might think this depends on whether you are giving or getting information, but it doesn't correlate as neatly as that. Talkers learn by watching the listener's expressions and movements and by asking questions. They also talk more by verifying or repeating answers. Nontalkers send information nonverbally, which is the way most information is transmitted in face to face situations.

PERSUASION

How do you tend to convince others to think, act, or feel a certain way? Do you try to give them hard, cold, logical facts that lead to the conclusion you wish them to come to, or do you try to manipulate, to play on the emotions by eliciting sympathy, fear, or anger, etc.? Perhaps you consciously try all of them or fit them to the person and the situation.

FOLLOWERSHIP

How do you tend to treat those with more power than you in the organization? Are you generally inclined to please or do you find yourself more often rebelling, either overtly or covertly?

CONFLICTS

How do you meet your need to deal with interpersonal conflicts? Do you confront them openly, perhaps even aggressively? Or do you tend to avoid conflicts, or if involved pretend they don't exist?

GROUP ACTIVITIES

How do you tend to function in group situations? Are you more on the active side, either to dominate or just for attention? Or are you more passive and noninvolved unless drawn out?

There are many other needs that we have and that are expressed in various stylistic ways. None is good or bad, but highly relevant to the situation and how you are perceived by others in the situation. This doesn't mean you can't generalize about your overall style or that you shouldn't learn about your styles and consider modifying them to function participatively. You should; it is part of knowing yourself. But rather than tinker on a unilateral basis, try talking about your styles, their influence and how you feel about them with someone you feel comfortable talking with and who understands the styles concept.

The primary reason for being concerned about styles and how others perceive them is this: people tend

to view other styles in terms of very simple values---
good or bad. We tend to feel comfortable with and
respectful toward people whose values, perceptions,
needs, and particularly styles are similar to our own. It
is difficult to be objective about others, even for those
who work at it.

I like to ask seminar participants how they think
leaders and followers with radically different authority-
related styles would describe each other. The answers
are always the same, in that they are expressed in
negative terms: dictatorial, wishy washy, overly dependent, smart aleck, hard to lead, no leader at all. It
becomes quite apparent from this exercise how important perceptions are and why you should talk about them
with people who are important to you.

Requirement #3- Skills, techniques and procedures that
encourage participativeness.

DEFINING ROLES AND FUNCTIONS

Defining roles and functions is the cornerstone of
participative management as it is for any other kind of
management. As a manager, you are primarily concerned with getting work done through others. This means
dividing up the work into logical specialties either along
traditional lines or with variations that suit your organization. The trick for our purposes is not only to get
people to accept responsibility for their function, but
also to be concerned about all other functions. Our
natural inclinations to mark off territories, compart-
mentalize, and stay out of the other fellow's backyard,
when carried to the extreme are detrimental to participation.

A logical design is still an essential foundation of
any organization. If you would prefer a biological
analogy, you need a skeleton upon which you can develop
a nervous system, glandular system, and muscle system
that will help the skeleton be sufficiently flexible to

meet any contingency. You can't build a body without a skeleton and expect it to stand up in the world.

COMMUNICATING POSITION RESPONSIBILITIES

A Position Responsibilities Chart lists all the things a person should know and be able to do to meet his/her obligations to the organization. Unfortunately, very few organizations have these devices that are so useful for recruiting, training, evaluating and all the other inter- active management activities. They are also useful to promote participativeness because they aid the commu- nication process between leader, follower, and peer. Participation means working together and this is much easier when everyone understands just what it is that they and others are responsible for. The need for the kind of communication that the Position Responsibilities Chart fosters is easily uncovered by asking a leader and a follower to describe the five to ten most important parts of the follower's job and approximate amount of time that he/she should spend on each. As noted earlier, the lists will rarely match or come close to it even in organizations that are proud of their internal communi- cations.

IDENTIFYING AND DEVELOPING KEY PERSONAL RE- LATIONSHIPS

Identifying and developing key personal relation- ships in the organization is another important skill of a prince(ss) who would be participative. The skill is difficult for some to master because it is hard to become completely objective about distinguishing between people who merely give pleasure and those who are really important. It may be necessary to separate your organization concerns from your non-organizational feel- ings if you want the organization to be successful. This requires a careful analysis of each relationship you have in the organization and a determination about the extent of their importance, and what you have to do to keep the relationship positive as well as productive. There are techniques you can use to improve your important relationships such as those described in Chapter 6 in this book. They all, however, come down to mutually surfacing and dealing with the relationship in an open, trusting way.

TIME MANAGEMENT

Time management is another key skill for the participative prince(ss). It is also a key skill for every other person. I mention it here only to emphasize that participativeness can increase efficiency and productivity but it seems to take more of the time of the prince(ss). I say <u>seems</u> because he/she will tend to spend more time with people and, incidentally, doing a lot more listening than telling. If your mind-set says that a prince(ss) directs and/or works on things or projects rather than through people, it will seem that you are spending a disproportionate amount of time in meetings.

IDENTIFYING PROBLEMS

You will have to be skillful in identifying those problems and issues in your organization life that are so-called "people problems" and in distinguishing them from those that are technical problems. Trying to train people to do the impossible or to do something that requires excessive dedication is as bad as trying to solve a problem with more money or machines or information when your people don't know how, or don't want to do the work.

SETTING GOALS AND OBJECTIVES

Setting goals and objectives for oneself and helping subordinates to set theirs is widely accepted as sound leadership practice. People like to know what their prince(ss) is after. People want to help the powerful, sometimes too much so. In their eagerness to be helpful, they frequently fail to question the wisdom of the basic idea, and that's not what participativeness is all about. Even in relatively casual organizations, it is helpful to have personal work goals and objectives tied into position responsibilities and freely communicated up, down, and across the pyramid to those who can help you.

One more thing about goals and objectives. They don't have to be end results; they can be set in terms of efforts. Goals and objectives have often been used as whips and clubs and as proofs of incompetence or indifference. There may be some justification to this approach if the person has complete control over all the factors that can contribute to his/her attaining the goals and objectives. Failure, then, may justifiably be attributed to lack of personal skill or motivation and whatever penalties received could be warranted. Quite often, however, the wherewithall to achieve goals and objectives is not under the person's control. In such cases, it is better to consider efforts or attempts rather than end results. This goes for you as well as your subordinates. True, this practice can be used by the dishonest individual or group as an excuse for not achieving results. However, the trained and developed organization does tend to avoid both blame placing and excuse making because of the freedom to take risks and be open about shortcomings.

THE MISSION STATEMENT

Goals should also be meshed into the mission statement of the person, unit, and organization. The mission statement is the shortest possible way to state the main purpose and function of a person, unit or organization. This is more difficult than it sounds and attempting to state a mission can launch an intense debate on the raison d'etre of the organization. It is a worthwhile activity because of the soul searching that it provokes.

Requirement #4 - Courage to overcome resistance from within and without.

You may know about the resistance to change in nature from the lesson in physics about kinetic energy. It says that a body set in motion will continue in the same direction unless influenced by another force. We all resist change in any number of small ways. If you naturally fold your arms with your right arm over your left, try to do it with your left over your right. If you normally put your coat on over your left arm first, try doing it over your right first. You'll notice a feeling of discomfort when you attempt to change even insignificant habits such as these. In varying degrees, we all like predictability in our lives which is just another manifestation of our natural fear of the unknown.

Powerful princes(ses) often appear eager to change things in the organization. What they really want is for everybody else to change, to fit their image of what things should be. Leaders, they'll explain, should be people of vision and should be able to motivate their people to become better than they think they are. The arguments are true when talking about running faster or carrying heavier loads or doing anything which is really more of, or better than, what they always imagined they were doing. It's not so true if we are talking about being concerned for the welfare and future of the organization and the people who are members of it, plus being concerned about being served by the organization and the society that surrounds the organization. It is not so true if you want members of the organization to be concerned problem solvers.

Some people do not want to participate and in most cases it would be a waste of time and effort to try to persuade them to. Others want to, but don't know how, or don't realize the price they will have to pay in terms of changing their ways. You personally are going to have many doubts about your own best interests and the way you serve the organization. You may sincerely and rightfully come to the conclusion that you are better equipped than all those around you to make decisions, and what's more, those around you may agree with you. It may be a very comfortable, acceptably productive symbiotic relationship. To attempt to change such a situation is going to take considerable faith in participation and in your case it may be misplaced and neither I, nor anyone else, can confidently say that you should be more participative at any given time. I can only predict with great confidence that being truly participative is going to take courage on your part.

Requirement #5 - Judgment regarding when to lead, when to follow, and when to collaborate.

The age-old concern of every prince(ss) who ever ruled, and every parent who ever parented, and every manager who ever managed is deciding when to let go and when to hold back. Behavioral scientists can develop elaborate models and techniques and teach them to serious students of leadership, who will seldom use them on a day-to-day basis. They will rely on the programs in their heads imprinted by role models and life experiences perhaps tempered by objective reasoning. It all comes down to a combination of intuition and thought and a measure of luck.

Letting others share your power and share your sense of responsibility for your portion of the pyramid is to opt for a certain belief in the ability and good will of those around you. It can lead you to an overconcern with the approach when it is the results that you are after, which would be a mistake. It can also result in an internal struggle. You may want to appear participative when everything in your makeup wants it to fail, in order to reaffirm your belief in your own superiority which would justify your being the prince(ss) and therefore worthy of the power and the prestige that goes with the status. This also would be a mistake. This brings us full circle back to the need for knowing ourselves. A variety of resource materials designed to help you think through your personal needs is described in Chapter 11.

The next chapter deals with the technology available to you to promote participativeness and increase productivity. It would help to start reading this material with a clear head about your needs as a participative prince(ss). But should you still not be sure about whether these needs have been met, read on anyway. Learning about the nature of the technology may help you to decide whether or not you wish to use it.

CHAPTER 5

THE ORGANIZATION DEVELOPMENT
TECHNOLOGY AVAILABLE TO YOU

OD stands for organization development which I define as: any planned activity directed toward helping the members of an organization interact more effectively as they pursue the organization's goals. OD is the science of objective cooperation.

Please note that when I talk about OD I am not talking about some other very important elements that influence an organization's success. For example, I am not talking about the physical settings and the concrete tools, materials and supplies your organization needs. Nor am I talking about external forces that influence your organization's performance such as economic conditions, political situations and environmental factors. And I am not talking about the more traditional technologies that an organization needs, depending on its specialization, such as engineering, production control, and distribution technologies. I am talking about people and the ways they think, feel, act, and interact in organization situations.

This relatively new and growing body of concepts, ideas, strategies, and techniques known as OD is the newest of the social/behavioral sciences. At this writing only a small percentage of princes(ses) of the pyramids in the world know about this new technology and the promise it holds for their organization's success. This is true despite the growing number of titles published each year on the subject and the fact that most major universities plus a host of minor ones offer courses and even degrees in OD. Other names that are either used synonymously with OD or overlap its scope include Human Resources Development and Organization Behavior. Courses that deal with OD technology can be found in schools of business, education, social science, medicine, and just about every other people-related field.

Many organization leaders would like to relegate OD to traditional organization departments. But as a leader there is no way you can have the benefits of this technology and relegate it to an individual, group, or department such as Industrial Relations, Personnel, or Training. It is something you must work with even though you may use specialists and consultants employed or contracted for that purpose. Power and OD must go together if either is going to serve the organization very well.

The OD definition we use is so broad that it would seem to take in just about any formal interaction between members of the organization, and in a sense it should. The difference in most organizations between OD and non-OD interactions is that the OD activities are planned with an understanding of human behavior and organizational dynamics in mind. The focus is on the human element rather than on the technical. It's not the budget in a budget meeting that is the focus of the OD effort, but the way the persons involved interact to get the budget developed, or trimmed, or accepted, or whatever the objectives of the interaction. That's why many OD people use the term "process intervention" to describe their efforts.

Until now, leaders who formed and led organizations had to rely on their own insights, intelligence, and common sense when dealing with the forces at work in organizational settings. While these qualities are still important, today's leaders can also draw on the growing body of OD concepts and techniques, and bring them to bear on the problems and opportunities of their organizations. OD has proven to be helpful in making organizations successful and in meeting the needs of everyone involved in them.

Here is a brief description of many of the techniques OD practitioners are currently using in all types of organizations. Some fit neatly into our definition and some seem to deal more appropriately with person/job interaction. Note also that some are only a few years old while others predate the OD title but serve OD purposes very well. While the list of techniques will change over the years, it would be wise for any participative leader to have at least a nodding acquaintance with the current names and the uses of the techniques described below.

Organization Diagnosis

Before a doctor or any professional problem solver prescribes solutions or treatments, he/she goes through a diagnostic step. We all know that. It is common knowledge in our culture. This two-step procedure is so logical that I hesitate attacking the use of it. But I must because it is not adequate when attempting to make your organization more participative through OD interventions. It is not the data gathering part that is wrong; that part is necessary and useful. It is the second part where the professional problem solver reads the data and decides what must be done that doesn't usually apply to organization development activities.

When gathering data for purposes of helping people to interact more effectively, it is important to remember that the data is best used as a mirror. Those involved can see things in the data mirror that otherwise would be hidden from them. This information gives them options for changing their behavior. Please understand that I am not denigrating data gathering as it is traditionally used by management to help make decisions. Even data about human behavior such as quits, fires, tardiness, pilferage, grievances, as well as financial data on expenses, costs, sales, and profits all can help tell the story of how people are performing and how productive the organization is. These figures tell the real story of productivity and in many cases should be the ultimate test of whether or not your organization development effort has been successful.

This "objective" or "hard" data can be of the utmost importance to you and your people as well as others. Only you can decide what is important to you. I couldn't begin to list what all the possible success criteria might be for the readers of this chapter. That's why I choose to concentrate my efforts on the gathering and use of data by the members of the organization whose behavior, thoughts, values, and feelings are reflected in the data. This data can then be fed back to the members of the organization in a way that they can understand what it represents and thereby gain new options about how to change their behavior.

It is important for you or anyone interested in the organization to grow "new eyes" if you are to function effectively as a participative leader. Perhaps you have heard the story of how three persons viewed the Grand Canyon and saw different things. A holy man saw the majestic work of God. A scientist saw the story of the formation of the earth's crust, and a cowboy saw a horrible place to lose a calf. We usually see what we have been trained or conditioned to see by our life experiences. Since few leaders have been trained or conditioned to lead participatively, they need retraining to help them see their roles differently.

OD data is usually collected and used in small doses within relatively short periods of time. The huge, detailed computer processed survey can yield useful management data, but it is not the most useful form for organization development purposes. The shorter the report, the more easily it can be understood, and the quicker it can be fed back to the participants, the better.

Another characteristic of OD data is that it can be considered factual only in the sense that the facts are perceptions by those involved. They are not objectively verifiable facts. Just assume that real truth doesn't exist or at least is unattainable by mere mortals. Then believe that you can gather facts about how one or more persons see and feel about the various factors that make up their organizational lives. This information can be tabulated and fed back to individuals who can see the extent that their perceptions are similar to and different from others. This helps people to understand each other, and provides a basis for discussion and negotiation.

There are as many different diagnostic devices as there are thinkers about organization behavior. I personally use more than ten different ones for different reasons and on different occasions. The instrument that I find most useful for uncovering perceptions is based on the S x C x T x M = I/OP formula described in Chapter 3 which helps to illustrate the interdependence of the many variables that are necessary to achieve maximum productivity. This organization perceptions instrument does not cover such things as profits, expenses, production, and the like. It covers performance factors, not the end results. If we were interested in end results rather than processes, we would have no need to determine and expose the perceptions of those involved. We would just go to objective measures such as those provided by the accountant.

Organization diagnosis, then, is done in a very special sense: not to determine objective truth, or even come close to it, but to determine perceptions since it is from perceptions that we can learn what people want and need. We can start where they are then and proceed to improve the situation. More of the organization diagnostic instruments I use are described in Chapter 11.

MBO or Management by Objectives

This technique is sometimes referred to as management by results, or both objectives and results. It is a system for integrating organization members' long and short range goals with those of their units and the entire organization. The MBO concept has been widely adopted with very mixed results. While the logic is hard to argue with, the application is often mismanaged. Without a powerful Orgeist, MBO can be used as a club by managers to hurt others or defend themselves simply by dealing with the letter of the law rather than the spirit. In the ideal MBO program, everyone participates in setting their own goals and the goals of the organization. Everyone knows at all times where they are going, why, how they are going to get there, what their progress is at any given moment, and how their efforts integrate with the efforts of others. MBO can be wonderful, but remember that a mechanical system, regardless how perfectly designed and administered, may fail when imposed full scale on an organization. Rather, it should evolve and grow in a more organic way, from the roots up.

Team Building or Group Development

This is probably the best known and most often identified OD technique or device. The process has roots in group therapy and while it still deals with the perceptions, feelings, and problems of individuals, it is now usually more often applied to helping the group to function more effectively on behalf of the organization. Typically, a group of 5 to 15 with some organization reason for being a group is trained and developed to solve problems and/or plan and execute projects. The well-trained and developed group, whether it is composed of top executives or first-line workers, deals simultaneously with five areas of interaction: their immediate environment, the content of any given problem or project, an operating structure of the members' own choosing, a logical problem solving or planning procedure, and group processes. The last item refers to the members' dealings with each other in an open, honest, collaborative way so they can have confrontation without hurtful conflict. They learn to accept themselves and each other, to make their conflicts creative, and their cooperation, despite difference, sincere regardless of the mixture of organization ranks represented in the group. Much more about this in Chapter 7.

Value Analysis

This technique is used to help people identify those things they feel strongly about. Values influence behavior. By identifying your own values and the values of others, you can learn to deal with them in an open fashion. This activity leads to more tolerance among members of an organization and enables each one to confront each other on issues that are normally emotion arousing.

Contracting

This technique helps people to become more aware of their responsibilities to each other. Contracting is usually used in one-on-one situations. As in any legal contract, both parties openly express what they will do in the future under certain circumstances that concern the other person. While this type of contracting is not spelled out in legal detail, the message and the expectations are clearly communicated. Contracts are made constantly between people who understand the concept for purposes of helping their interaction become more productive and more harmonious.

The Mission Statement

This is a short, succinct statement that capsulizes the purpose and intent of a dyad, group, department, or the entire organization. Usually the process of discussing, developing, and agreeing on the statement is more worthwhile to those involved than actually having the written statement. In most organizations and subdivisions thereof, the mission is assumed to be commonly accepted when in fact it seldom is. It is usually a very worthwhile first step in the development of a group.

Long-Range Planning and Goal Setting

This process is a matter of setting realistic, attainable, and measurable objectives to the extent that it is practical to do so. Any unit of any level in an organization can do this, but it is most important for the top group. The measurability factor provides a way to read the extent of progress, and to develop soundly requires the input of all knowledgeable members. Communicating the goals to all members serves to galvanize them into a common effort. Progress reports serve as individual and group reinforcements.

Attitude Surveys

Surveys have long been used by social scientists to study organizations and the feelings that members have about various aspects of the organization. They are used as a basis for unilateral management decisions. Quite frequently such survey reports have done nothing more than serve an academic interest. They sit collecting dust on shelves in many executive offices. When used as an OD technique, the attitude survey findings are freely fed back to the participants and the problems and the opportunities uncovered are offered as something that both management and members can work on. OD surveys, as mentioned earlier in this chapter, tend to be smaller and acted upon with greater speed than the traditional attitude surveys.

Org Development

An org is a unit or cell of an organization composed of a leader and one of his/her followers and the follower's job situation. The three elements make up the org and are useful for identifying and dealing with these relationships. The org development process is a matter of training both the leader and the follower to understand how they each view the relationship, and then training them to negotiate differences within the confines set by technical, practical, and policy considerations. More about this technique will be explained in Chapter 6. A full explanation of how the insights gained from analyzing helps a leader in the recruitment, selection, training, directing, counselling, coaching, evaluation and motivation of individual followers is presented in People, Power and Organization. It is also used as a basis for a management course called "Management by the Individual" that my organization offers.

Behavior Modification

One fact that behavioral scientists can prove repeatedly is that rewarded behavior tends to be repeated. The anticipation of what a reaction will be is the major influence of the actions people take. On the job this means people will do their jobs better and be generally more productive if their behavior is appropriately rewarded. It sounds simple, but there are some important additional "ifs" that must be understood. Your people can become more productive through behavior modification techniques if they perceive the reaction for their accomplishments as the reward, and if the reward immediately follows their productive behaviors. Behavior modification is sometimes seen as contrary to the spirit of OD because if done unilaterally, it can be considered manipulative and one sided---dangling a carrot in front of the donkey kind of approach. However, it can be done participatively by involving the members of the group whose behavior is being modified in identifying the more productive behaviors and choosing the rewards and the manner in which they are given.

Norm Modification

This OD strategy is based on the view that much of organization member behavior is governed by group norms. Norms are those unwritten behavioral rules that group members follow and that may or may not contribute to achieving organizational goals. When negative norms such as "Everybody steals a little around here," can be identified and replaced with positive ones, such as "We all respect the company's property here," the members and the entire organization benefit.

Job Enrichment or Job Enlargment

This is a technique for broadening the scope of a person's job to provide greater variety and challenge. The technique is based on the belief that work itself is a motivator for many workers, and excessive routine and boredom result in underutilization of the worker's talents, poor performance, and general discontent. Putting a clerk in charge of an entire mailing rather than just addressing envelopes would be an example of job enrichment. While not technically an OD intervention, it can be if those whose jobs are enriched are involved in the redesign of the job and its evaluation.

Sociotechnical Redesign

This is a technique for structuring the work environment, and specifically the work processes, to meet human needs. For example, jobs that can't be enriched or broadened due to tradition, economic, or efficiency reasons, may be made more palatable, even challenging, by installing systems for letting the worker constantly measure his progress as he does his work. The farmer who put a colored stake every hundred feet so pea pickers could see their progress as they worked what otherwise seemed like endless rows of peas is an example. The technique is similar to behavior modification, but comes before the behavior pattern has been established.

Force Field Analysis

This technique is used for systematically reviewing and anticipating all the forces that may work for or against a change or a proposed course of action in the organization. By identifying these forces, you have a better chance of dealing with them before battle lines are drawn, and peace, in the eyes of those involved, is considered secondary in importance to being right or winning. Intelligent use of this technique can help promote "win-win" situations where everyone with a power base in an organization cooperates and benefits. It is a natural step in the problem solving and project planning process.

Conflict Resolution

This refers to a group of strategies for helping conflicting individuals or groups within the organization to surface their feelings and expectations about each other and interact in an open, problem solving way. The strategies are usually quite simple, but their effect can be profound.

Intergroup Merging

This is a technique for helping the members of merged groups integrate. They learn how to recognize new power relationships, group standards, norms, and interpersonal expectations. In short, making one group where two existed before, with loyalties toward the previous group gone and feelings of cohesiveness with the new group strengthened.

Interpersonal Feedback

In an OD context, feedback is an interpersonal communications technique originally used in encounter groups to help members to become more sensitive to their feelings and those of others. The technique involves reacting to others nonjudgmentally. You do this by telling them the impressions you have of them, the behaviors you observed that gave you the impression, how you feel as a result and what you intend to do about it. Interpersonal feedback is given in a spirit of welcoming feedback in return for purposes of promoting mutual growth and understanding.

OD Team Development

This is the process of identifying those members of the organization who seem to have a natural proclivity for OD efforts. The process includes recruiting and training those individuals in OD concepts and techniques and helping them to become either direct or indirect agents for positive changes in the organization's processes.

Multiple Management

This is a relatively old and unknown organization design for fostering better communications and utilizing human resources. The traditional pyramid structure is maintained to distribute responsibility and authority but peer level councils are used to solve interdepartmental problems "informally" and to provide a two-way channel of communications for policies, ideas, and information. The councils are made up of representatives of various levels in the organization.

Training

Training is not usually considered as an OD strategy, mostly because it is hundreds, or perhaps thousands, of years older than OD. Indeed, the training field was one of the major fonts from which OD has sprung ---the others being clinical psychology and management. Perhaps it would be truer to say that OD sprang from a recognized weakness in management and human relations training programs. All too often, changing an individual through traditional training methods is lost in a very short time once he/she returns to the original organization environment.

Training given within a systematic framework of an OD program tends to be more lasting. When everyone in the organization receives the same general training, they have a common frame of reference from which they can constantly reinforce one another in their day-to-day interactions. Thus, the training is constantly reinforced by group norms.

Training efforts such as those specifically designed to develop supervisors or managers to handle their subordinates can readily be fitted into our definition of OD. The concepts of OD can be profitably used in training programs for public and customer-contact people and for members who must work effectively with many individuals in various departments or sections of the organization. Such programs have traditionally been called human relations training programs, but are currently being updated with behavioral science techniques. The most popular model for such training programs is TA---Transactional Analysis. This concept enables the trained person to identify the ego state (parent, child, or adult) that all persons involved in an encounter are using as they interact, and to deal with each effectively. Such training is frequently a part of an Internal Consultant Development Program.

Sales Organization Development

Selling, in the minds of many, is inextricably associated with competitiveness and therefore contrary to OD principles. Beating the competition and outproducing your fellow salespeople is usually the common ideal among those who accept the challenge of a sales career.

Sales organizations can become more competitive externally if they can become more cooperative internally. This is particularly true of industrial-type sales organizations. Sales organizations that must cooperate with other company departments and specialists have long known the value of fostering the spirit of objective cooperation. This is also true of salespeople who are most successful when they establish long-term problem solving relationships with customers and other salespeople as well as other key people within the organization. A characteristic of sales organizations that practice organization development techniques is the formation of councils or groups in each level of the sales organization. These groups meet to solve mutual problems and to communicate up, down, and across the organization pyramid. This practice can overcome the debilitating competitiveness and distrust that is so characteristic of many sales organizations.

Sales Group Development and Group Selling

If your organization now sells big ticket or very expensive products or services to large volume accounts, you already know that the job of the super salesman, like the superstar and the Lone Ranger are myths of the past. Big time selling, like big time buying is a team effort. Salespeople need help from people in marketing, research and development, engineering, production, and even top executives. Sales groups can be formed on a permanent or temporary basis to attack a particular marketing challenge. Such groups can be trained and developed to be many times more effective than the best salesperson or the untrained group. Such groups can plan and execute effective marketing strategies for a single account or an entire area. It brings out the best balance, the best approach through a combination of creative conflict and objective cooperation.

Internal Consultant Development

A consultant is someone with specialized knowledge and skills that a client works with to solve a problem or to realize an opportunity. Many specialists in large organizations function more effectively when they feel, behave, and are treated like they are consultants. Specialists in such fields as accounting, engineering, safety, data processing, training, purchasing, and quality control should be considered as consultants rather than service people or experts. The line organization is rarely best served by getting just what it wants from specialists or blindly following an expert's advice. More about this in Chapter 10 which covers working with internal and external consultants.

Organization Planning

This is a technique for structuring the organization and creating the most effective and convenient departmentalization within the organization. The technique involves examining the total work requirements of the organization and assigning duties, responsibilities, and tasks to every functional area of the organization and to every individual. It usually involves the development of job descriptions for every management position from the chief executive officer to the first-line supervisor. It also involves the development of policy statements for all major activities of the organization. The technique predates OD but integrates nicely into the entire organization development concept.

Human Resource Planning

This is a technique for determining how many people the organization will need in the future and in what parts of the organization they will be needed. It also predicts the types of skills that will most likely serve the organization and the kinds of people the organization will need to provide for smooth, continuous growth.

Brainstorming

This is a group idea-producing technique that has long and successfully been used in creative fields such as advertising. It is used in OD programs to teach individuals to work with each other in a non-critical, non-competitive atmosphere. It is part of the problem solving and project planning process.

PERT or Program Evaluation Review Technique

This famous technique for planning and illustrating the complex interactions of the various parts of a large undertaking was born in the aerospace industry and has applications to OD. PERT graphs show with great precision the interdependence of the persons and groups involved in a project. It can be a powerful aid in fostering objective cooperation because each person can see what every other person and group is responsible for.

Planned Meetings

Meetings can be used for the traditional reason of giving and getting information, but may also be engineered through format and seating to foster feelings of mutual respect and equality among the participants. Schoolroom-like meetings, for example, promote teacher and pupil attitudes, whereas round-table meetings tend to promote peer attitudes.

Career Planning

This is an organization-sponsored effort to help individuals plan their long-range and short-range goals, particularly future positions and jobs in the organization. Usually a committee or group of individuals interviews and sits in and otherwise helps an individual candidate plan where he/she wants to go in the organization. The assumption here is that the individual is and will be a member of the organization and is looking for ways to improve him/herself in the organization as well. This kind of program tends to foster loyalty and openness, and thereby strengthens the bond between the individual and the organization.

Labor/Management Committees

The development of groups composed of local management and local union leadership dates back to World War II and is now a rapidly growing phenomenon in plants and warehouses across the country. These committees deal with real local issues that are beyond the scope of traditional collective bargaining, without impairing or compromising either party's negotiating position. The group works on internal communications, conflict prevention, performance improvement and the quality of work life. This kind of group development effort is an OD intervention that can have immediate, dramatic, and measurable cost effective payoffs for the individuals and interest groups involved.

Information Systems Analysis

This is a method for looking at the way messages are formally transmitted through regular channels and informally transmitted through the well-known grapevine. What messages are sent, how they are sent, who sends them, and who receives them all influence the organization in an integrative or disintegrative way. Redesigning the formal system and learning how to use the informal system can reduce unnecessary friction and promote cohesiveness.

Troubled Employee Program

At any given time, five to ten percent of the population needs help with emotional problems. These troubled individuals manifest their problems in alcoholism, drug abuse, poor work performance, and personal conflicts. Organization executives, managers, and supervisors can be trained to identify troubled employees and encourage them to use inside or outside helping services. This type of program may be considered as an organization development effort.

Quality of Work Life

This phrase, often referred to as QWL, is used by some writers as synonymous with Organization Development. Others use it to refer to only that aspect of OD that deals with the needs of people. As a name it has the advantage of greater receptivity by workers because it seems to emphasize their interests.

In summary, OD is a relatively new science/art/-profession that holds a great deal of promise for participative leaders. As humans we have the age-old need to be considered as individuals and to be members of one or more organizations. Organizations are the vehicle through which all of us will improve our lot in the world. Leaders have always recognized the importance of the organization phenomenon, and have more than others struggled with its problems. At present, only a small percentage are consciously employing the OD techniques described in this chapter. However, in the near future, these strategies and those still being developed will be common tools of the participative prince(ss).

Perhaps the greatest promise of OD lies in the fact that the importance of meeting the needs of all organization interests, members as well as owners, clients, suppliers and society, is becoming more widely recognized. This is true not only because individual members are important to the success of the organization, but also because as individuals we recognize our responsibility to be concerned for each other and for each other's needs. The literary arts have often led the social sciences, as illustrated by this famous line written by John Donne in the early 1600's: "No man is an island entire to itself." OD can help the participative prince(ss) make his/her organizations more successful in meeting the needs of all interests and individuals and in helping them to achieve their productive potential.

CHAPTER 6

THE VITAL RELATIONSHIPS
IN YOUR ORGANIZATION

Relationships in this book refers to how people feel and act toward one another. The relationships within an organization that can legitimately be termed vital would be those that have a direct or nearly direct impact on the organization's success. The success of these relationships is naturally related to the success of the organization. Relationships are more important in organizations that are relatively less structured, where the members must frequently interact to solve problems or plan and execute projects. In other words, they are more important in non-routine situations. In heavily structured machine-like organizations, relationships are of lesser importance because production can be controlled by the structure itself---whether it is imposed by fiat, technological necessity, or social norms.

This chapter should heighten your awareness of the many relationships in your organization and their importance to its performance. You should also gain insights into origins of your relationships, their current status, and how you might develop them.

Developing relationships is an essential skill for the participative prince(ss). Your personal happiness and that of your people are as dependent on your relationships as is your personal and organizational productivity. How we relate to others undoubtedly has as much to do with whether we feel good or bad as anything else in our lives. Unfortunately people usually blame the other person for an unhappy relationship. This is true despite the well-publicized and sound view expressed in the phrase "I'm OK, You're OK," immortalized by Dr. Harris, in the book of the same name. In many cases, it would be more realistic and instructive to say "I'm OK, you're OK, but our relationship is lousy."

There are four types of relationships that can be described as vital to the organization. The first type is relationships between individuals and are called one-on-one, dyadic, or interpersonal relationships. The second is individual/group relationships. The third is intragroup relationships, and the fourth is intergroup relationships. There are other relationships that can be very important to an organization that will not be covered because they are not exclusively internal to the organization which is the prime focus of this book. These are relationships such as buyer/seller, contractor/subcontractor, regulatory agency/regulated persons or departments, or any other relationship that necessarily involves members of the organization with non-members.

One-On-One Relationships

The leader/follower relationship is actually just one formal variation of the more powerful/less powerful type of relationship. Like all such relationships, it is based on the thoughts, feelings, and experiences of our past, particularly our parent/child experiences. This is the power relationship we all have in common, even if our parents were not our biological parents. Anyone who served as a parent figure served as our role model for exercising power.

Our behaviors in such relationships tend to fall into a pattern or style. When we are the most powerful party, we tend to either exploit, ignore, or be protective of the weaker party. When we perceive ourselves to be the less powerful, we tend to either avoid, rebel against, or submit to the stronger party. We also tend to be open or secretive about our perceptions of the relationship. No style should be considered as good or bad, other than how it make the parties feel and how it helps or hurts the organization achieve its goals.

The way people perceive and feel about the person they report to in an organization, and the people who report to them, is of paramount importance to individual

and organization performance.   Incompatible persons
tend to avoid contact.   Obviously, this can have dire
effects on work performance.   Leader/follower mis-
matches produce disproportionate numbers of involuntary
terminations, absentees, tardies, grievances, and thefts.
They also produce low quality work in general. Compati-
ble leader/follower relationships have the opposite
effect: people feel better, they produce more, and it
costs less to keep them on the payroll.

The leader/follower relationship is fully covered in
my earlier book, People, Power and Organization.   The
relationship between the two parties plus the follower's
job situation is termed an Org, and is presented as a unit
or cell of the organization.   The Org is illustrated by a
model with three scales---each representing degrees of
structure. The scales are used to plot the leader's style
and the follower's style, and the follower's job situation.
The extent that a leader tends to impose structure is
plotted on the first scale. The extent that the follower
tends to prefer externally imposed structure is shown on
the second scale.   The structure inherent in the job
resulting from organization rules, technological necessity
or other factors is plotted on the third scale.

An Org pattern is developed by marking the
location of each element on their respective scales and
connecting them as indicated by the broken line in Figure
1. Research has shown that relatively vertical patterns
mean better interpersonal harmony and higher productivity. Irregular or nonvertical connecting lines as shown
in the example, means the opposite. It is very important
to note that there is no absolute way to place an
individual on the scales. The position is dependent on the
perception of the person viewing the relationship.   But
perceptions can be important information to both parties. Allowing a leader and a follower to illustrate how
they see each other and their relationship in an objective, non-threatening way sets the stage for discussion,
negotiation, contracting, and ultimately improved performance.

FIGURE 1

The model used to illustrate the Org Concept

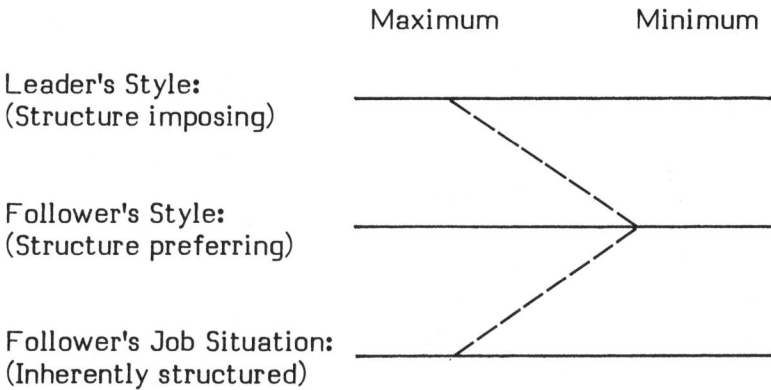

	Maximum	Minimum

Leader's Style:
(Structure imposing)

Follower's Style:
(Structure preferring)

Follower's Job Situation:
(Inherently structured)

The Org concept is as far as I know the easist way to help leaders and followers understand their relationship and to guide whatever corrective actions that may be necessary. It helps to use self-scoring instruments plus exercises to facilitate the development of the relationship. These items are described in Chapter 11, under Leader/Follower Relationship Development.

Peer relationships are also one-on-one and involve members of the organization who are of the same rank and who theoretically hold the same amount of position power. Of course it is possible for peers to have different amounts of other types of power. Power can be obtained through having special skills, special knowledge, special access to powerful people, the exclusive use of resources, or by possessing special personality traits. Peer relationships may be two people who work for the same boss, in which case they are frequently referred to as "siblings". Should they have the same rank but work for different bosses they would be more like "cousins," but are also referred to as sibling relationships in the material that follows.

The origins of our thoughts, ideas and feelings about sibling and cousin relationships within the organi- zation are probably based on our life experiences with our real siblings and cousins. In our culture, siblings tend to have rivalrous attitudes toward each other as well as with their cousins. However, many such relationships are supportive and characterized by mutual defense and strong interpersonal loyalty, particularly during times perceived as threatening to both parties. It is safe to say that sibling and cousin relationships, whether real or representational, are more volatile than others. The parties can be comrades one minute and at each other's throats the next.

The best way to keep sibling relationships both positive and productive and to quickly resolve conflicts should they arise, is to help the parties understand the nature of their relationship: help them to understand why it may be volatile and how they can surface and talk about the pressures that influence their behavior, making one or the other relatively dominant or submissive, competitive or cooperative, or even destructive of their own best interest and the organization's as well. This can be facilitated by an objective third party, say, their prince(ss) or a competent consultant. Here too, it helps to use special materials so the parties share perceptions of their relationship, surface their problems, and deal with them in an adult way. Forms, exercises and materials that aid in the development of various peer relationships are described in Chapter 11.

The simple model on the next page is used to illustrate how one organization member perceives his/her relationship with another member in terms of their relative power in the organization and their feelings about the relationship.

FIGURE 2   -   Interpersonal Relationship

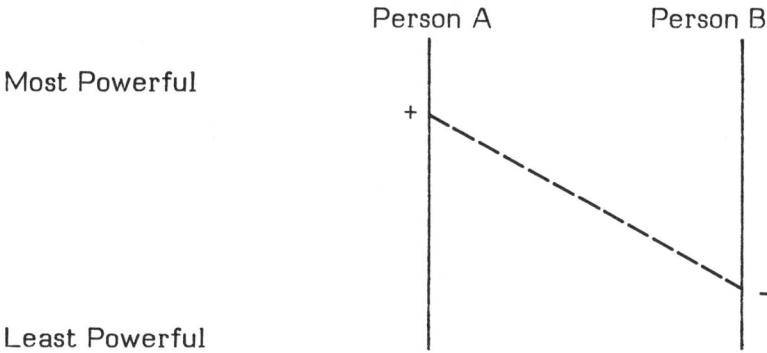

In this example the person completing the model (broken line) sees A as very powerful in the organization and B as much less powerful. The plus sign indicates that he/she believes A views the relationship as relatively pleasurable and productive while B feels more negative toward the relationship.

Another interpersonal relationship that is important to the organization is that between specialist and user, usually a staff specialist and a line department member. I prefer to call them client-consultant relationships. This particular relationship, when it refers to an Organization Development practitioner and the leaders of a client organization, is treated extensively in Chapter 10. In this chapter I am talking about any organization member working in a temporary capacity with another member as a helper. Increasingly, large organizations are designating certain internal specialists as consultants. These specialists may work in data processing, training, engineering, finance, purchasing, or any other technical area, and are usually on call to various line executives. Characteristically, these specialists are looked upon as part-time employees whose functions are to do the user's bidding. In some cases, the user relates to the specialist as very sick patients tend to relate to their doctors. "I'll do anything you say---just save me." Neither the dependency nor the exploitive relationship is conducive to solving complex problems where both parties have a stake in the relationship and the project being worked on.

Internal specialists function better when they are trained to establish objective, trusting, problem solving, peer relationships with their clients. This requires a certain self image and the interpersonal skills necessary to establish an adult relationship with a person who may consider him/ herself as relatively more powerful in the organization. Figure 3 illustrates this concept.

FIGURE 3

Specialist/User Relationship Model

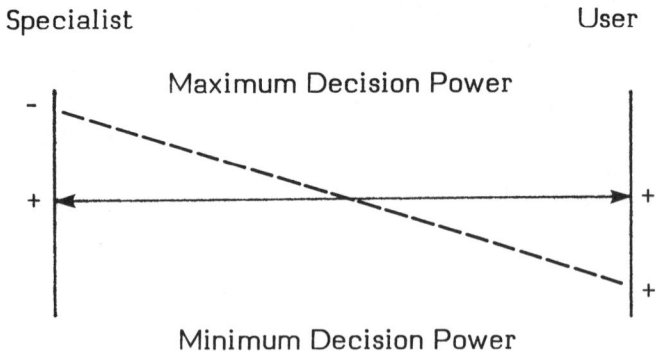

Specialist   User

Maximum Decision Power

Minimum Decision Power

The person completing this model used a broken line to illustrate his/her perception that the specialist is currently making nearly all the decisions regarding a project being worked on for the user. The plus indicates he/she believes the user likes the arrangement and the minus indicates the specialist doesn't. The horizontal line with the arrow ends and the plus signs represent what the relationship should be in the opinion of the person completing the model. The parties in this type of a relationship can express their perception of it by using the model individually and then comparing what they have drawn and explaining their perceptions. Models such as this can help to illustrate something that is abstract and dynamic and thereby promote cooperative, objective discussion about the relationship.

Individual/Group Relationships

It is useful to think in terms of an individual/group relationship when either the individual sees him/herself as distinctly apart from the group and/or the group tends to have a collective view of a particular individual. There are many opportunities for relationships like this to develop in organizations with more than a few members and can be of great importance to the organization.

The most common individual/group relationship is one involving a prince(ss) and the people who report to him/her. The most commonly accepted models of leader and follower interaction treat subordinates as a group. This is no doubt because the ancient and traditional organization models had a group of people performing the same tasks under the direction of an overseer. In a great many modern work organizations it is more common to find the followers working independently and doing a great variety of different tasks. For this reason I prefer to think in terms of "Management by the Individual" rather than "Management by the Group." I use the former term as a title for the Management Development Program which my associates and I conduct for clients. Please make special note of what I mean by this, because later you may read something that sounds somewhat contradictory. When a manager is directing or leading a subordinate, it is best that he do it on a one-to-one basis. That is what I mean by "Management by the Individual." However, a group of subordinates meeting with their manager can be very useful for exchanging information and for solving problems. This will be covered more fully under Intra-Goup Relationships.

Another common individual/group relationship found in large organizations is that between a powerful executive and a unit or department of key technicians such as attorneys, engineers, chemists, accountants, educators, and so forth. These relationships tend to engender "he/she against us" feelings and also tend to be negative. Of course, these "power/expertise" conflicts must be avoided and if they exist should be surfaced and dealt with. If ignored they may very well lead to bad feelings and less than full cooperation. While position power will usually win out over expertise power, it may not be in the best interest of the organization. Win/win thinking must be the guide for both parties.

Countless variations of the individual/group relationship that do not involve position power can be found in the large organizations. Most often they involve a new person in the group. They usually are of short duration, lasting until the individual is integrated into the group. Even short-term discomfort, however, can be an impediment to progress and very expensive to the organization. The new kid on the block can be cocky and try to make the group over to his liking or he/she can try to learn the group norms and assimilate as peacefully and as quickly as possible. Similarly, the group can "kow-tow" to the new charmer or exclude him/her from unofficial membership, even if they can't deny him/her official membership status. The group can also gang up, wolf-pack style, and attack the individual to drive him/her away or force him/her to conform to group standards. Non-acceptance can be crushing to some as can demands for complete conformity. If assimilation cannot be both quick and pleasurable for all, it is usually best to abort the effort because the organization is bound to be the loser.

The final individual/group relationship that I think is important to mention is that between the most powerful person and any group in the organization. As mentioned previously, and as noted by other writers since the time of Caesar, first line soldiers like to see their general walk among them. The natural halo that

surrounds the most powerful person can become tarnish-
ed when not exposed to the gaze of the rank and file. It
is comforting to know that your ship is sailing under the
direction of a captain who is both competent and caring.
If you have ever experienced a long, perilous voyage, you
know how you longed for someone whom you could relate
to and who knew how to handle the situation, and who,
despite all the problems, cared about you and was
accessible for guidance and comfort.

Intragroup Relationships

Intragroup relationships are important to the organization's success as well as to the feeling of well
being and worthiness of individual members. By definition, a group is two or more persons who recognize their
membership in the group. Americans historically tend to
denigrate groups and glorify the individual. It would be
hard to find a member of a large organization who didn't
have something negative to say about committees.
Complaints center on the slow pace of groups and the
little they seem to accomplish. No doubt we can all say
this with justification because nowhere is more time
wasted and more irritation generated than in group
meetings. Yet we also know that the synergism of an
effective group can accomplish more than the individual.
When the situation is complex, several informed people
can muster more resources, ideas and skills to solve problems or plan projects. Of course, most groups are not
naturally effective. Fortunately, it is possible to help
groups become extremely effective through specialized
training and development. However, the job usually
requires a person with the talents, tools, and techniques
to do the job.

To simplify things I tend to label groups in terms of
the power of the members. There are leader/followers
groups, peer groups, and mixed power status groups. I
use power as a criterion because it is power that tends to
influence the workings of a group more than any other
factor. This is not so true in groups formed for the sole

purpose of giving and getting information as it is for groups formed on a temporary or permanent basis to solve problems or to plan and execute projects.

Groupings of individuals who work in close proximity to each other and who interact and meet often are quite common in most sizeable organizations. They are usually composed of a prince(ss) and those who report to him/her and are usually known as staff meetings. The meetings are considered as a tool of the leader for purposes of giving and getting information. Normally, the leader sits at the head of the conference table or in front of subordinates which tells everyone where power and control really lie. This form of meeting has many uses and will no doubt be with us for a long time. The weakness inherent in the practice becomes apparent when the leader wishes to use the group to help solve a complicated problem. The power of the leader tends to corrupt the problem-solving process. While some leaders are able to "hook" their people out of their normal subordinate role and into an "equal" frame of mind, most people and most groups have trouble attaining this mode without special training and development.

I suggest that groups, even after training and development, use a special symbol to indicate that a leader has voluntarily given up his position power for a period of time, so that the group can work on a problem or project uncontaminated by the power issue. The symbol I prefer is a small cube or box, imprinted with processes and procedures for problem-solving. It is placed on a table and prominently displayed during the problem-solving sessions, and taken away when the leader wishes to resume his role as the most powerful person present. More about the training and development of groups later in Chapter 7.

It is helpful for the members of a leader/followers group to understand its purpose and nature. It is also helpful to see themselves as others see them in relation to the group. A model such as that shown in Figure 4 can be useful when illustrating how members perceive the influence that the other members have on the leader, and vice versa.

FIGURE 4

Leader/Followers Group Model

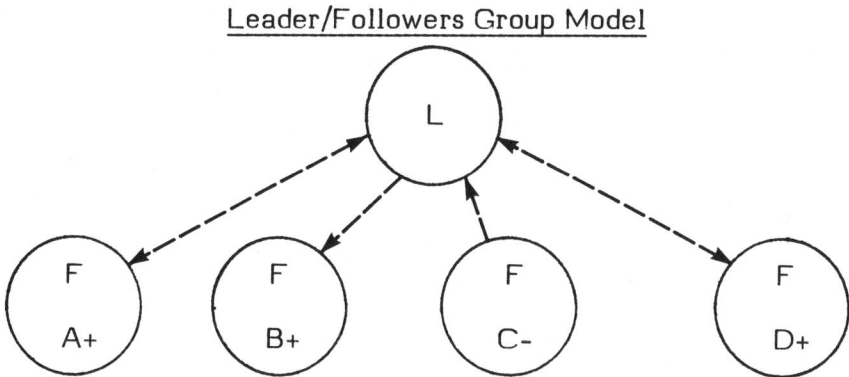

In this example the person completing the model (broken lines) perceives that follower A influences the leader and is influenced by him. B is essentially a "receiver" and is influenced more by the leader than he influences the leader. C is an influential person who is somehow managing to influence the leader more than he is influenced by the leader, and D, like A, operates in a give and take mode with the leader. What is good or bad for this group will depend on what the leader wants and how productive the group is. There may be good reason why one or the other group member is more influential than the others. The + and - signs indicate how the perceiver believes the parties feel about the relationship.

Peer Groups

Peer groups or groups of mixed power status, whether they are permanent or temporary task teams, can have relationship problems that influence their effectiveness. A great deal will be said about training

and developing groups in Chapter 7. Here I would just
like to emphasize that intragroup relationship issues can
be surfaced and group members can be shown how to deal
with them.   This benefits the organization and the
individual members.

        The model shown in Figure 5 is used to illustrate
how one member sees the dynamics of a particular group.
By comparing perceptions the members can learn to
modify their behavior to deal more effectively with each
other.

FIGURE 5

Peer and Mixed Rank Group

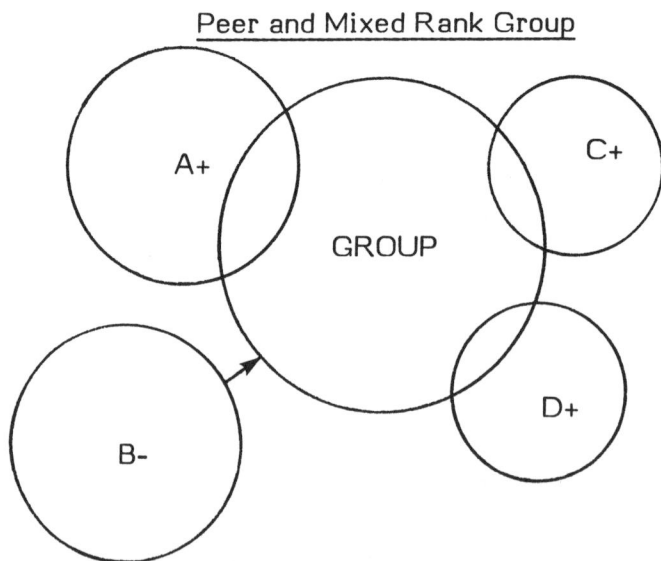

        This model consists of a large circle identified as
the group.   The person who completed it has added
smaller circles, letters and signs. He/she sees members
A and B as relatively more powerful people, but while A
is interacting effectively with the group, B is only giving
and not being influenced by the group. C and D are less
powerful, as indicated by their size, but both are giving
and taking from the group, as they should. The model is

useful for depicting how one person sees the relative power of the members and the extent that they are giving and taking from the group. The + and - signs indicate how the perceiver believes the individual members feel about their relationship to the group.

Intergroup Relationships

The last category of vital relationships is called Intergroup Relationships. Conflicts between groups in large organizations are probably more common than among individuals within groups. Perhaps it is because we have a racial memory of the era when we lived in tribes and were constantly threatened by other tribes, and, therefore, have a natural tendency to think of our group as the good guys and the other groups as the bad guys.

Conflicts among official groups in the organization, such as between various departments, may be based on the fact that the members have different value systems. They may be owner, client, member, or society-oriented as described in Chapter 1. Or they may be more self- or other-oriented as described in Chapter 3. In any case, the group members tend to sincerely believe that only they are acting in the best interest of the organization and the other group is self-serving. For example, conflicts between the sales and the credit department are traditional because the self-serving behavior of one tends not to serve the self-interest of the other: e.g., sales to less than credit-worthy customers.

Frequently there are conflicts among unofficial groups which are those not designated to fill an organization function but that exist for some "cultural" reason. Examples would include groupings of people who identify themselves as white collar or blue collar, union or non-union, shift one or shift two, plant one or plant two, male or female, older workers or younger workers, home office or field office, line or staff, new members or old timers, premerger or postmerger, and so on, ad infinitum.

It is usually in the interest of top management as well as the organization to mitigate tribal loyalties or group identification unless it is used in a very adult and positive manner. This would have to be an acknowledged bowing to a natural proclivity to form groups to which we are loyal, and consider more virtuous and superior to other groups. Competition between groups to boost sales temporarily or collect more money for a charity drive or to play on the company softball team, may have an overall beneficial effect on the organization. In most cases it will be wise to play down all rivalries and encourage people to learn and accept the principles of cooperation. Every member should be ready to form new groups for a temporary effort such as our pioneer forefathers did when they formed trains of covered wagons to help each other move westward.

Intergroup development activities can also be useful when combining two groups such as executive teams of merging companies. Old interpersonal relationships and pecking orders must be erased and new loyalties developed so the new group can emerge and be prepared to serve the organization, rather than dissipate their competitive urges with attendent feelings of being an "in" or an "out".

Intergroup development can also be of benefit to sibling groups: those engaged in the same general activities. The performance of sibling groups can easily be compared, even though they may be in differenct locations or attached to different departments of a large organization. Developing the relationship between them facilitates the transfer of personnel as well as the exchange of information and ideas.

Developing the relationships of sibling groups that report up through the same hierarchy in the pyramid is easier because of the stabilizing power of the top person. Cousin groups are those under different leaders and, therefore, have less inclination to cooperate. Invariably it is in the overall best interest of the organization, if practical, to promote an open and trusting relationship with frequent interaction among both sibling and cousin groups.

The Intergroup Relationship Model shown in Figure 6 is useful for illustrating perceptions of intergroup relationships and for promoting an objective discussion about improving them.

FIGURE 6

Intergroup Relationship Model

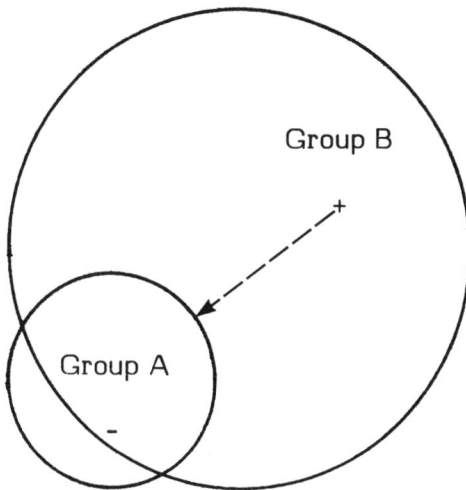

The person completing this model (with broken line and arrow) sees the B group as almost completely dominating or controlling the A group. The arrow indicates one way communication from B to A and little concern for the needs and thoughts of A. The plus and minus signs indicate the way the person completing the model believes the members of both groups feel about the relationship.

The secret of developing intergroup relationships is similar to that of developing interpersonal and intragroup relationships. First, assume that most people want to live openly, peacefully, and cooperatively with most others, particularly with other members of their organization. Despite this desire, many forces conspire to foster competitive attitudes that result in excessive time, energy, talents and techniques being needlessly spent on the relationship, rather than on the work of the organization.

With this view of the organization world in mind, it becomes obvious that positive interventions should be made in the interpersonal, intragroup and intergroup processes. These interventions should help the members of the organization recognize what is happening. They should be of such a nature that they encourage people through education, experience, and the support of powerful people, to surface their concerns and make plans to work together more cooperatively. This seldom happens naturally; it requires a systematic surfacing of what each party needs and expects from other members, plus a format for exchanging views, negotiating differences and contracting future behaviors to develop the vital relationships.

If you agree with me that interpersonal, intragroup and intergroup relationships are important to your organization, your course of action should be clear. You will have to identify the relationships that are vital to your organization. The official ones will be relatively easy unless your organization design is vague and generally unknown. The unofficial relationships may take some thinking about.

Your next step is to find out how the various parties in the relationships feel about the others, and if the feelings are negative, how negative? To put it another way, to what extent is the negative relationship detrimental to the organization? Finally, you will have to make decisions about how existing conflicts can be resolved and good relations strengthened.

As a prince(ss) you no doubt instinctively deal with many relationship problems on a day to day basis. You may even believe that such work is the essence of your job. After all, management is widely acknowledged as the function of getting work done through others. But keep in mind you are part of the system, and the development of relationships usually requires a strong sense of objectivity. I hope you recognize that seeking help in such matters is a sign of strength and not an admission of incompetence.

A final word of caution: most adults do not like to admit that they have prejudices or that they cannot get along with another person or group. Therefore, simply asking people about such things may not yield the truth. You may have to use objective instruments or an outsider who is skilled in obtaining information about the less than optimal relationships in your organization. But the solutions you accept and the decisions you make are yours. There is no way you can delegate them. Only you have the power to initiate beneficial changes and provide the sustained support to see it through. You must accept and retain ownership of the problem and the challenge of making all the vital relationships in your organization positive and productive--givers as well as takers to the Orgeist. The best way to develop good relationships throughout your organization is by systematically training and developing groups in your organization. The next chapter tells you how.

CHAPTER 7

THE TRAINING AND DEVELOPMENT OF GROUPS

I usually call them OD (organization development) groups simply because I have yet to uncover or invent a better name for them that is more descriptive of their function. Their purpose is to facilitate communications, develop the skills of the members of the group, solve organization problems, improve performance or productivity, develop proposals, and/or plan and execute projects.

They are not pyramid groups---meaning a leader and those who report to him for purposes of the usual staff meeting. I exclude these groups because they usually function as tools of the leader: tools he/she uses to discharge his/her responsibilities. As mentioned earlier, this is a useful and legitimate use of a group but it is not an OD group as long as the leader retains control to serve his own ends. They can become OD groups if properly trained and developed and if the leader agrees to "turn off" his power when the group is in session. Remember: power tends to corrupt group problem solving and planning.

It is not important whether you call your OD groups task teams, communication groups, project groups, problem solving units, ad hoc committees, or whether they are temporary or permanent. The important thing is that you and your people understand that the groups are a thing apart from the regular power structure. They are outside the pyramid but they emphatically do not replace it nor do they assume any of the power vested in various persons in the pyramid hierarchy. The decisions or actions of the group can be curtailed by the power structure at any time.

The purpose of OD groups is to serve the organization. This means helping the organization fulfill its mission, progress toward its long range goals and meet its short range objectives. They do this by working on problems or projects that are most sensible for them to work on. By sensible, I mean that marketing people work on marketing problems or projects, and finance people work on finance problems/projects, and so on. These assignments may be of the group's choosing or dictated by management.

It is important that groups be trained and developed to deal with problems/projects because the untrained group usually is ineffective, wastes a great deal of time and annoys people who feel they have more important things to do. Note that I constantly use the term "train and develop." The reason is that training alone--how to do it--is not enough. Many people know how to do things but do not do them because the organizational environment tends to inhibit, discourage or even forbid their using their skills. A developed group of individuals have learned skills together, appreciate and support each other, and generally encourage each other to use the skills and techniques they know lead to worthwhile accomplishments.

It is true that groups can develop naturally. Developed groups make sure their meeting setting is suitable, they adopt and use a reasonable structure, they follow a logical procedure and deal effectively with interpersonal issues and they are both effective and pleased with their work. Naturally developed groups like this are rare and are composed of unusually sensitive individuals. They probably have taken many meetings and months to develop. Group development techniques make the long lead time unnecessary. Any group of reasonable, normal people in a relatively stable organizational situation can be trained and developed to perform effectively as an OD group--to solve problems, plan and execute projects or develop and evaluate proposals--and enjoy doing it.

Group Training and Development Procedure

The general procedure I have found most successful for training and developing OD groups is this:

1. Determine membership

The first step is to decide who will be part of the group. A powerful person may make this decision or individuals may be consulted and invited to participate. As you might expect, members who are asked to form the group by their own leader or an even more powerful person tend to do so more willingly and with an open mind. When candidates are asked to join such a group by their peers, there may be much negatively tinged debate about the need or desirability of doing so.

The reasons for inviting or ordering any one person to join a particular group would naturally depend on the general mission of the group. Some considerations that should influence selection are: technical knowledge, internal and external contacts, the resources the person brings to the group, power in the organization, current information or expertise, skill in working with groups, objectivity, ability to understand the problems and opportunities facing the organization, interpersonal skills, and concern for the task at hand.

2. Interview each participant before the group development effort

Interviewing is best done by the internal or external consultant charged with training and developing the group. He/she explains the theory and practical consideration of the group development effort and deals with any misgivings and misconceptions the individual may have. He/she also tries to uncover information that will be useful in the development of the group and generally prepares the individual to participate with an open mind. The consultant is interested in the skill and knowledge level of each individual, his/her attitudes toward the consultant, the other people in the group and the entire organization. He/she is also interested in determining each person's expectations regarding the development effort and the group in general. Finally, the consultant is interested in the problem or opportunity areas the group can successfully deal with.

Various instruments may be used to gather data during the interview sessions, and pre-meeting readings or other assignments may be given to the individual to save precious workshop time and help prepare the individual to participate. It is important that the interviewee agree to attend or participate in the meeting with an open mind, at the very minimum. Hopefully, he or she will look forward to the experience as an opportunity for personal growth and satisfaction.

3.   Conduct a training and development meeting

The group development meeting may last anywhere from two to five days. Three consecutive days is usually adequate but other schedules may be used. The days tend to be long and intense so privacy and comfort are essential in a location. The agenda tends to be loose and rather poorly defined. This is because the consultant conducting the meeting maintains a certain flexibility to meet the group's needs as he trains and develops it. Basically, the agenda can be broken down into two large sections. The first is training and development and the second, for lack of a better term, would be group work. The training and development part is mostly exercises, discussions, and case work that helps the participants to accept the fact that groups are or can be more effective than individuals when problem solving. This part also helps to sharpen the group's problem solving, project planning, communication, and thinking skills. It also provides the opportunity to uncover and deal with interpersonal issues that influence the group's performance.

The second portion of the group training and development meeting is usually devoted to deciding upon the group's purpose or mission, and then identifying and prioritizing the issues, problems and projects that the group should deal with. Then the group actually works on one or more of them. The progress the group makes and the accompanying feelings of personal accomplishment experienced by the members provides an immediate pay-off for both the organization and the individuals involved.

Time during the meeting may also be spent on structuring the group and preparing it to perpetuate itself either indefinitely or for the term of the project assigned to it. This involves setting future meeting dates, choosing locations, assignments and other details.

The last part of the session should be devoted to evaluating the experience of the meeting itself. This should also set the precedent for all future meetings of the group. It is easy to slip back into old ways. The group should take the time to examine its performance. It will help to perpetuate the use of the processes and procedures, tools and techniques that prove to be useful.

Here is a breakdown or description of what an OD group must be trained and developed to deal with to become maximally effective.

Group Membership

In my opinion, the number in any given group should be between seven and ten, but as few as three, and as many as fifteen can be effective. Deciding who is to be a member should be determined on the basis of his/her potential value as a resource for the group because of the factors mentioned earlier in this chapter. However, people are sometimes assigned to permanent groups just so they can have a part in the group system or for their own training purposes. A person can be a valuable member of a group even if he/she is entirely ignorant of the subject matter to which the group is generally devoted. Members in either permanent or temporary groups can be of equal or unequal ranks, have the same boss or different ones. It all depends on the purpose or mission of the group. Of course memberships may change for any of a number of obvious reasons such as work load, transfers and so forth. It helps to have both analytical and intuitive people in a group. It also helps to have people with a variety of other personal and interpersonal styles. If the group has been trained and developed to not only be tolerant of unimportant differences but to use all members as resources, the experience can be very exciting.

Group Mission

Like an entire organization or any segment of it, an OD group should have a clear and concise statement of purpose that all members can understand and accept. In the case of a permanent group it may be general such as: "To handle all mechanical problems that develop in Production Facility Number 1." Temporary groups may be more specific: "Cut cost on Model 24A by 10%, within 30 days."

Problem or Project Content

Content refers to the technical aspects of the problem or project being worked on. It is the part that the untrained group generally concentrates on to the exclusion of the other elements. It naturally varies with the group and the problem or projects, so there is not much I can say about it here. When training groups, I use this heading to provide basic instruction about the difference between facts and opinion. To break it down even further I offer this progression: hunches, ideas, feelings, thoughts, opinions, anecdotes, hearsay, testimonials, logical deductions, direct observation, verifiable facts, repeatable proofs.

Work Setting

Work setting refers to the actual physical location of the group when it is engaged in problem solving or project planning. Modern technology permits members of a group to be many miles apart and communicate through telephone or videophone and even transmit documents electronically, but most groups meet in person, and I suspect the face to face setting will always be more effective. The environment should be conducive to the free exchange of ideas along with sufficient order to reach the objective. Some suggestions are quite obvious. The room should be private, have adequate lighting, ventilation, comfortable chairs, writing sur-faces, and sufficient space to get up and move around, if necessary.

Flip charts and markers are preferable to chalk boards and overhead projectors. The sheets can be hung with masking tape on the walls and referred to easily. Some OD practitioners prefer not to have tables or anything else that suggests a barrier between people. For problem solving I prefer a table, but one that is either round or square, or a series of rectangular tables that can be arranged in a large U or square so that all members have easy visual contact with all others.

Structure

Structure refers to the basic organization of the group and the meeting. It is structure that prevents the meeting from being a bull session but when overdone can inhibit the creativity of the group. The elements of structure for OD groups include: the roles played by various members, the time limitations, the agenda, and any rules that the group adopts to govern its behavior.

It is important to have a leader or moderator of the group who understands that his/her power is quite limited. His/her job is to lead the group through the selected procedure for each item of the agenda and to regulate the flow of talk. This job is more like that of a referee and the leader must not take advantage of the role to push his/her views. A facilitator may also be used. The facilitator is concerned with the interpersonal and group processes that tend to help or hurt the group as it works on a problem. Well developed groups may not need a facilitator because the group is self facilitating. This means that the members are sensitive to positive and negative processes and intervene when necessary to prevent the group from being counterproductive. These processes will be discussed later in this chapter.

It shouldn't matter who the chairperson or moderator is. The role is not difficult and anyone can learn it quickly. In permanent groups it is best to have a system of rotating chairpersons so everyone gets a chance to set up the meeting, prepare the agenda, and so forth. Here is a list of suggestions for the chairperson.

Before the Meeting

1.   Distribute "draft" of agenda with the meeting announcement.

2.   Distinguish "problem" items from "information" items.

3.   State problems in terms of questions: "How can we...", etc.

4.   Invite agenda improvement suggestions before the meeting.

5.   Suggest ways the participants may prepare for the session.

During the Meeting

1.   Use a flip chart to show agenda.

2.   Invite comments on the agenda---additions, dele-
     tions, combinations, priorities and time allocations.
     Agree before proceeding.

3.   Post chart pages showing the procedure to be
     followed and the Negative and Positive Processes.

4.   Select a facilitator. He or she will be most
     responsible for keeping the processes positive, but
     all participants should facilitate.

5.   Watch the time and lead the group through the
     agenda using the appropriate procedure.

6.   End the meeting with individual action plan reports
     from all participants on what they plan to do as a
     result of the meeting.

7.   Lead group to decide on arrangements for the next
     meeting.

8.   Have the facilitator discuss and evaluate the
     group's performance during the meeting and allow
     others to do the same.

After the Meeting

1.   Send copies of reports to all interested parties
     covering:

     a.   Basic data on make-up and mission of group.
     b.   Problems or projects currently being worked
          on.
     c.   Progress Report.
     d.   Current assignments of group members.

2.   Do your assignments and encourage others to do
     theirs.

Procedures

Procedure refers to the sequence of logical steps a group takes to fulfill its function. They need not be strictly adhered to but serve as a very useful guide. There are a number of procedures offered by various writers on the subject. I offer procedures for the following:

> Performance or Productivity Improvement
> Creative Problem Solving
> Corrective Problem Solving
> Preventive Problem Solving
> Project Planning
> Proposal Development
> Proposal Evaluation

As you will see, all of these procedures are basically problem solving activities because they all deal with going from some present condition to some desired condition. If they seem to be too long or complicated, think of the remark made by the famous writer, H. L. Mencken: "To every complex problem there is an answer that is simple, neat, and wrong." Problem solving in all its variations is usually a difficult, tedious, and time consuming activity. Group problem solving may be slower than individual problem solving but the solutions tend to be better because the group usually has more information and other resources to draw upon, and because of the synergistic effect of group work. Implementation of solutions involving the actions of group members also tends to be more effective because the individual members develop a feeling of "ownership" for problem solutions and therefore strive harder to make them work. Here are the procedures:

The Performance or Productivity Improvement Procedure is used when the group is concentrating on doing certain tasks or jobs more efficiently.

1. Describe present performance or production in numerical terms--X results per Y expenditure.

2. List steps in present procedure.

3. Set a tentative goal for improvement:
    Mini---the minimum target gain and
    Maxi---the most that can reasonably be expected.

4. Evaluate each step in present procedure in terms of
    the extent it contributes to the end result.

5. Brainstorm variations in entire procedure and in
    each part.

6. Critically examine each new idea presented.

7. Formulate a new procedure.

8. Devise a way to test the new procedure.

9. Test it and keep records.

10. Revise as necessary.

11. Involve all concerned in the adoption and imple-
    mentation of the revised procedure.

The <u>Creative Problem Solving Procedure</u> is used
when the group is working on a "How can we..." or
creative thinking problem. Or when the group is dealing
with some opportunity that may not even be considered a
problem such as "How can we most profitably invest one
million dollars?"

1. Determine objectives

    The more specific, attainable, and measurable, the
    better the chances of attainment. Start with "How
    can we..." Guide with: Who, what, why, when,
    where?

2. Identify obstacles

    Whatever is likely to inhibit attainment of the
    objectives.

3.   Inventory resources

     List everything that could be useful in overcoming
     obstacles and reaching the objectives.

4.   Brainstorm ideas and approaches.

     Anything goes, upside down, backwards, inside out,
     combine, enlarge, shrink, compress, divide, etc.
     Defer judgement. Use creative thinking.

5.   Evaluate options.

     Consider pros and cons, relative costs, potential
     payoffs.
     Use critical thinking.

6.   Decide by consensus.

     Sincerely seek full agreement before resorting to
     majority rule.

7.   Plan to implement

     Make assignments. Who will do what by when.

8.   Try it, test it

     Expect the unexpected, stay flexible.

     REPEAT THE PROCEDURE AS OFTEN AS NEC-
     ESSARY.

     The Corrective Problem Solving Procedure is used
for "What went wrong..." types of problems. It is used
when trying to find a malfunction in a complex mechanical process or any well established system, to get things
back the way they were.

1.   Describe what the situation "should be." Try to use
     quantitative terms.

2. Describe what the situation "actually is" and "is not."

3. Gather data related to differences between what should be and what actually is. When did it change? What events preceded it? What clues can be found? Who was involved?

4. Massage the data, play with it, analyze it, look for patterns, correlations, unusual facts.

5. Brainstorm all possible causes.

6. Evaluate each idea critically. Prioritize in order of their probability and test if possible.

7. Brainstorm possible solutions.

8. Evaluate ideas.

9. Decide on actions to be taken, their order, and alternate courses of action based on various contingencies.

10. Plan who will do what by when.

11. Try - test - evaluate each attempt.

REPEAT PROCEDURE AS NECESSARY.

The Preventive Problem Solving Procedure is what a group does when everything is going well but wishes to be prepared for anything that might happen to spoil or change the present situation. This procedure is sometimes referred to as Contingency Planning.

1. Describe in quantitative terms what is happening now. Answer the questions who, what, why, when, where, how, and to what extent?

2. List components or functions in time or operational sequence.

3. Identify dependencies---what does each major component need to operate?

4. Evaluate relative reliability of essential components. Find the weak link.

5. Brainstorm possible back-up measures to strengthen weak components and/or replace them in the event of failure.

6. Evaluate various backup measures and decide the order in which they are to be used should a breakdown occur.

7. Prepare to act. Assemble resources and train key persons to use them.

    REPEAT PROCEDURE PERIODICALLY.

    The Project Planning Procedure is followed for such undertakings as introducing a new product, moving the organization to a new location, or changing over to a new power source. These are problems in the broad sense but are usually considered as a normal part of many jobs and, therefore, the term "problem" may not seem appropriate to many.

1. Organize project team.

2. Analyze known facts and discuss opportunities.

3. Develop project objectives.

4. Generate several general strategies.

5. Project probable consequences for each considered course of action.

6. Decide on most promising series of steps.

7. Identify, prioritize, and schedule specific tasks.

8.   Estimate minimum/maximum resources needed.

9.   Design a control system.

10. Anticipate and prepare for objections and resist-
     ances to plan.

11. Present the proposed plan to those with power.

12. Negotiate approval and cooperation of the power-
     ful.

13. Recruit, train, and direct project personnel.

14. Obtain necessary equipment, supplies and facilities.

15. Lead and coordinate implementation efforts.

16. Respond appropriately to behaviors that are helpful
     and harmful to the project.

17. Evaluate progress and revise plan if necessary.

18. Report final results to all concerned.

The Proposal Development Procedure is used to
develop the group's recommendations to other persons or
groups.   The final proposal may be written, spoken,
visualized, or any combination of the three. The intent
is to persuade others to make the recommended decision.

1.   Target person or group:
     Determine who really has the power to say yes, no,
     or maybe to your proposal. This is your prospect.
     The others may be influencers or gatekeepers and
     may also be important, but keep your eye on the
     real target person or group.

2.   Prospect's needs:
     Find out what he/she fears losing, or hopes to gain.
     What gives him/her pleasure or pain in these areas:
     technical, organizational, personal, interpersonal,
     quality, price, delivery?

3.   Attention:
      Make sure you have your prospect's undivided and
      favorable attention.

4.   Conditions:
      Develop a series of statements that will be easy to
      agree with and that will make your prospect aware
      of the problem or opportunity, confident in your
      ability to deal with it, and that will stimulate
      his/her desire to bring the situation to an agreeable
      conclusion.

5.   Label:
      Give your basic concept or idea a brief, descrip-
      tive, and catchy title.

6.   Describe:
      Tell in simple sequential steps how the idea should
      be implemented.

7.   Explain:
      Tell how the steps described above will bring
      benefits that will meet your prospect's needs, or
      solve his/her problem. Anticipate the most likely
      objections and explain them away before they are
      raised.

8.   Make acceptance easy:
      Give your prospect an easy, but positive way to
      commit to your proposal---a small step or a choice
      between two equally committing steps.

9.   Leave the door open:
      Indicate your willingness to further discuss and
      negotiate if it is necessary and feasible to do so.

      The Proposal Evaluation Procedure is used during
the critical review of suggestions, recommendations or
offers presented to the group. The proposals may
originate from individual members of the group or

outsiders such as vendors, other groups, or individual outsiders. The procedure can also be used by a group to evaluate the proposed solution it develops in a creative problem solving session.

1.   Verify needs:
      Is the proposal of real interest and value to you?

2.   Review logic:
      Does the flow of reasoning seem based on facts and not opinions?

3.   Identify actions:
      What specific steps will you have to take if you agree to the proposal? What will these steps cost in money, time, effort, reputation---and other items of importance?

4.   Quantify all benefits:
      What will be gained if everything happens as proposed?

5.   Compute return on investment:
      What is your net gain if you get and give as specified?

6.   Estimate certainty:
      To what extent can you be sure you will get what you bargained for? Consider performance history of proposer, references, built in penalties for non-performance, and external conditions over which neither party has control.

7.   Compare cost benefits with other proposals and other courses of action.

8.   Brainstorm:
      Think of ways to improve the proposal.

9.   Decide on a counter proposal or acceptance and submit to original proposer.

Communication Skills

When training and developing OD groups, it is usually helpful to include work on basic communication skills. Of course this depends on the background of the participants, but a review of the basics of giving and getting information accurately plus interpersonal feedback for dealing with emotionally charged communications usually proves to be useful. The handout I use to provide basic instruction in these areas contains the following information:

A. Communicate completely---cover all bases, let people understand you by giving them information on any important issue or problem by telling them:

  1. Your perceptions---what you see, hear, smell, touch and feel.

  2. Your interpretation or judgments---based on your perceptions.

  3. Your feelings---positive, negative, or mixed.

  4. Your intentions---what actions you will take now or in the future.

  Help the other party explain their views by careful listening and questioning.

B. Communicate congruently---try to make your words match the non-verbal messages you send.

  1. Voice---tone, inflection, delivery.

  2. Facial expressions and eye contact.

  3. Body language---posture, movement, use of hands, gestures.

  4. Time, location--when you choose to talk, where, under what circumstances.

5. Actions---what you actually do during conversations and after.

C. Feed forward---transmit information appropriately.

   1. Consider your receiver's values, feelings, perceptions.

   2. Obtain "favorable" attention.

   3. Make your statements clear, logical, sequential.

   4. Speak from the general to the particular, and from the known to the unknown.

   5. Try not to speak down or up to others.

D. Factual feedback---request responses from your receivers and use to regulate the flow of transmission. Listen, really listen, and observe gestures and behaviors. These may be one or more of the following:

   1. Signal of understanding, such as a nod. (Least reliable form.)

   2. Repeating what you said.

   3. Restating what you said.

   4. Giving verbal examples, analogies and applications.

   5. Answering and asking questions.

   6. Actual performance or demonstration that proves the message was understood. (Most reliable form.)

E.   Group discussion

1.   Respect roles of chairperson and facilitator.

2.   Summarize or otherwise feed back understanding of previous speaker's message and have it affirmed by him/her before making your statement.

3.   Don't allow your statements to be ignored, passed over or unresponded to if you believe a response is necessary or helpful to you and the group.

Processes

This refers to the interpersonal interactions and group dynamics that influence the effectiveness of a group. They are usually subconsciously initiated, responded to, and perpetuated, and can be classified as negative or positive, depending on whether or not they help or hurt the group as it pursues its mission.

NEGATIVE PROCESSES

Indifference or Disinterest

This means a person just doesn't care what the group is doing and includes not participating, looking out the window, or at his/her watch, reading or doing something other than what the group is doing. Note that I said these behaviors indicate an indifferent attitude. The person may look disinterested and not be. That is why it is important for a facilitator or another member of the group to stop the proceedings and confront the person about his/her apparent disinterest. When the matter is cleared up, the group can proceed either without the person or with his/her participation.

Misuse of Power

Power is misused when the leader or most powerful person behaves as though he/she believes his/her view should prevail. He/she can intimidate others by inter-rupting them, stepping on their lines, or putting the person down in any number of ways that say, "Don't forget I am more powerful than you and I plan to use my power to get my way." Conversely, someone who continually defers to or opposes those with more power is also misusing power. Remember the objective in OD groups is to use the combination of talents in the most objective and complete way to solve a problem or plan a project. Powerful people must agree that when they are participating in an OD group, their power is equal to that of other members.

Goal Setting Avoidance

This is a very common negative process. Setting goals is the hardest part of problem solving. It can be tedious and time consuming. The temptation to argue over some minor point is strong. It takes discipline to spell out the objectives in precise, measurable terms. Doing so, however, enables the rest of the procedure to be followed with relative ease.

Hidden Agenda

This is the term used to describe ulterior motives. Members of the group that seem illogical or stubborn in either supporting or opposing a specific point may have a reason for doing so but don't wish to reveal it. People can play dumb, but if the entire group is trained to recognize when a member has a hidden agenda and how to confront him/her, they can deal with the matter. If the real issue cannot be dealt with, there is no use in trying to solve a problem because the non-helping member will be working against a successful consensus. Of course, this can be even more difficult if the person with the hidden agenda happens also to be a powerful person.

Rivalries and Subgroupings

When people line up against each other for emotional rather than logical reasons, there is no hope for the group to become maximally effective unless the rivalry can be surfaced and resolved.

False Unity

This is a misuse of <u>esprit de corps</u> that makes people feel they must project a united front. It tends therefore to inhibit opposing viewpoints from being expressed. Hence, objectivity is lost and decisions are made on an emotional basis.

Holding Back

This refers to members not participating, either through shyness or for some ulterior motive. Holding back deprives the group of the resources of one of its members. Those who hold back usually justify their non-participating with statements like: "I don't know much about this" or, "When something starts happening that I don't like, I'll speak up - don't worry." These are not acceptable responses. Even those who are relatively unknowledgeable about the topic can participate through questioning, facilitating, brainstorming, and other procedural activities.

Assumptions of Inferiority and Superiority

These are similar to the misuse of power but refer not so much to position power in the organization but to the power people have in groups because of their experience, vocabulary, speaking manner, size, or anything that tends to make people listen to them more than to others. Women are well aware of the fact that deep masculine voices tend to get more attention in groups then feminine ones. Untrained groups commonly follow the advice of the person who seems to be expert on the subject. This can be very dangerous. Experts can make the most fundamental mistakes, just as non-experts can.

Experts should be used as a resource, but they also should be made to explain why they believe as they do, with no excuses about it being too technical to explain to laymen. They should never be followed blindly simply because they are recognized as experts.

Digressions

Getting off the subject is a very common phenomenon in untrained groups. It is usually justified on the grounds that the digression deals with subject matter which is important to the group and the organization. However, if it is that important, it should be put on the agenda and time set aside to deal with it. Try to stick to one subject, one problem or project, at a time. Of course minor breaks for tension relieving humor or casual "points of information" can be accepted with no significant loss to the group's effectiveness.

There are a number of other negative processes that would seem to require no explanation. Some overlap others mentioned but the terms are useful in describing what is taking place. They include: negativism, defensiveness, closed mindedness, manipulative tactics, overly concerned with time, not really listening, suppressed feelings, nit picking, being too easily satisfied, avoiding the hard work and tensions some projects require, excessive kidding and wisecracking, and being overly critical, or overly concered with the proceedings and processes.

POSITIVE PROCESSES

Positive processes are any conscious or subconsciously directed attitudes and behaviors that tend to help the group communicate and achieve its mission and goals. Group members should be sensitive to them, practice them and encourage their use. Here is a thumbnail description of the more important ones.

Goal Committment

This means being really concerned with setting and achieving goals. This motivation is necessary to take the time, tension, and energy that goal setting sometimes requires.

Concerned Objectivity

This term is meant to convey the need for an appropriate combination of the emotion that comes from commitment and the mental objectivity necessary to accomplish the job. I refer to it as the "Orgeist".

Openness, Being Upfront, or Leveling

These qualities are akin to honesty. Letting people know how you think and feel encourages others to behave similarly. People are usually relieved to discover that exposing themselves, their thoughts and feelings, elicits empathy and the respect of others. It helps also to get down to real issues and avoids much of the game playing that goes on in untrained groups.

Sensitive and Supportive

People working together in groups tend to become friends and therefore concerned with each other's needs. They want to help each other contribute to the group and feel good about it. They learn what helps and hurts other people. Frequently, they change their behavior to fit their new understandings. They do this by actively listening when others speak, by exhibiting a cooperative spirit, and by seeking ways to resolve conflicts with win/win techniques so that no one feels they are losers.

Confrontive - Risk Taking

Trained group members have no qualms about being confrontive and taking risks. This means letting others, particularly powerful people, know when they disagree or suspect a negative process, such as a hidden agenda, is at work. (Well trained group members know that conflict is inevitable when a group is made up of people with different viewpoints, needs and values and they are working on an important problem or project.) They also know there is such a thing as creative conflict, in which people can agree to thrash out issues without attacking each other.

Consensus Seeking

Perhaps the most useful positive process a group can utilize is consensus seeking. Consensus means that everyone actively agrees to a decision before it is made. In typical staff meetings the leader usually makes the decisions using varying degrees of input from the others, depending on his style and the norms of the organization. Leaderless peer groups usually settle things democratically through a vote which may be explicit or just implied because no one objected when one or a few people supported a certain decision. Silence is commonly considered an agreement.

Trained and developed groups work very hard at trying to get complete agreement such as a jury does. Members are trained not to succumb to peer group pressure or agree just for the sake of relieving tension or getting the job over with. Those with minority views have an obligation to stick to their position as long as they believe it is right. They also have the obligation to explain why they believe as they do and not just stubbornly hold on to their views. Similarly, majority position members have the obligation to explain their views and to really listen to minority ones. The realities of a situation may necessitate making a decision based on majority rule, but all members should be aware that this is a compromise and second best to a consensus. It is true that voting is quicker and we all are culturally conditioned to accede to the wishes of the majority, but let's not forget that although this method is a politically sound way of dealing with differences it is not the best way to solve complex problems or develop complex projects.

Clarity

When an OD group is in session, it helps to have the agenda, the procedures to be followed, and the negative and positive processes posted so that all may see and refer to them. The posting of these chart pages can be a symbol to the group that certain rules apply, that position power is temporarily suspended, and that they are obligated to use their time and talents to deal objectively with their problems or projects to the best of their ability.

Further Suggestions for Group Development

The group may decide to adopt any structure, format or procedure they wish and work on any problems they wish or one that is assigned by management. The group should be considered as an organization asset just as if it were a computer. In reality it is a form of computer made up of several individual computers, and very valuable ones at that.

Of course people and groups are much more than computers and capable of doing more for the organization than a computer ever will. It is also important that each individual recognizes that group work is one of his or her major responsibilities to the organization. Members of new groups sometime complain that they are too busy with their "real" work to devote so much time to group work. I like the answer of a company president I know who responds to such complaints with, "Tell me what you are doing that is more important then solving problems for the organization."

People learn more about themselves, their co-workers, their co-workers' functions, and many things about the organization in the process of working with a group. When they are chairpersons of their group, they learn a number of useful leadership functions. In addition, the chairperson role fosters contact with other groups and powerful people in the organization. It thereby provides a method of gaining favorable attention and exposing one's talents to others in the organization.

Part of the group training and development process usually includes techniques and strategies for working with other individuals and groups in the organization. This phase covers deciding who is likely to oppose and who is likely to support various activities and what the group can do to foster acceptance and negotiate their project to a successful conclusion. This takes special tools, techniques and training.

I would like to end this chapter by emphasizing the importance of the trained and developed group to the participative prince(ss). The OD group is the most visible expression of the Orgeist. It is where the action is. It is a vehicle for objective cooperation. It proves to all that you want participation---that you want to hear what everyone has to say on important issues without being committed to following the group. You retain control and everyone understands this. In actual practice you will find that the group, if given the right data, will most often make the right decision. The group is the nuts and bolts of participation, a most important element in making your organization maximally productive. Train and develop your groups well and give them the support they need to perform. They will do wonders for the organization while building a sense of personal worth in the heart of each member.

A number of instruments, exercises and other materials useful in the training and developing of groups is described in Chapter 11.

Techniques for integrating the individual groups into the entire organization is the subject of the next chapter.

CHAPTER 8

DEVELOPING A NETWORK OF GROUPS
WITHIN THE PYRAMID

In this chapter you will read about methods for weaving your permanent and temporary groups into the fabric of your organization without upsetting the traditional pyramid structure. True, the groups form a sort of substructure and they gain some power---meaning the ability to influence the organization---but the distribution of position power need not be disturbed. As a matter of fact, the official power structure of the organization may be strengthened because of the fact that reporting relationships will become better known and understood.

Types of Groups

Let's look at the groups that become part of the network. Primary groups formed from various departments in the organization will usually be the most numerous and the most permanent. Members may all work at the same location or at many different locations. Ideally, every member of the organization should belong to a primary group made up of people who perform the same general function or interact closely and regularly. In family terms they would be siblings or close cousins. Whether the group is composed of peers or members of mixed rank shouldn't really matter once the groups are trained and developed to deal with position power.

Permanent special function groups may also be part of the network. These are groups that are permanent but composed of non-power-related individuals. Committees with responsibility for safety, new products, development, engineering review, government affairs, ethics, or anything else that usually has an ongoing and indefinite life span belongs in this category. Groups usually not part of the network are the unofficial ones. These groupings may spontaneously develop and attract the old, young, experienced, new, short, tall, black, white, language A, language B, location X, or location Y, profession pi, or profession rho groupings. Unofficial groupings are usually negative or neutral in regard to their contribution to the organization. They can be a counter-productive force and should, therefore, be well integrated into the various official groups. If the organization has the right Orgeist, the need for unofficial groups will be obviated. The individual members will be able to satisfy all their needs that are usually fulfilled through group or tribal membership by participating in their official group. They will have a channel of communication to the power centers in the organization. They will have the opportunity to grow, contribute, be recognized, and they will have the companionship of their peers. They will have a distinct identification within a social mechanism that is specifically designed to overcome the naturally divisive influence of unofficial groupings.

In very large organizations, interaction of the many groups with the top executive group becomes difficult, if not impossible. Some organizations have dealt with this problem by forming representative groups or councils from each level of management, and various technical specialists and workers in major locations. Membership is on a rotating basis and the representatives report to their constituents and to management, but otherwise function as any of the smaller problem solving or project planning groups.

There are some other very important benefits to be gained by forming a network, but first I will define more precisely just what a network is. A network in the OD sense is a collection of independent units that can initiate activities and invite other units to participate if appropriate. This means that a group may deal with a problem or an opportunity that is entirely within its own province or with issues that involve changes for others outside the group. For example, the payroll unit may decide it needs a new item of equipment, the cost of which is within the discretionary budget of the most powerful person in the group. Naturally, he/she simply makes the purchase. The problem is solved with few people outside the unit aware of the change. On the other hand, suppose the payroll unit decides that a new method of gathering data from all departments is in the best interest of the organization. The group would no doubt have to secure the approval of management and then introduce the new system throughout the organization. The group could also seek support for developing and installing the system from other groups in the network. However, if the group can only develop ideas and must rely on the power structure to introduce it, unnecessary resistance may develop and this certainly is not the OD way. On the other hand, inviting debate on an issue that could easily be introduced and accepted in a routine manner may delay the project unnecessarily. Judgment will always be necessary when making decisions about human social systems and will always carry an element of risk. However, a knowledge of OD principles, experience, confidence, and sincerely attempting to do what is right for all organization interest groups minimizes the risks.

Once again, despite the presence of the network of OD groups, top management and the pyramid's power structure never gives up control. The groups are told from the start and reminded often that unless they are given a specific project, their job is to solve problems within the scope or mission of the group. On other issues they must sell their ideas or seek the support of the powerful. Admittedly, much of this must be worked out through trial and error and much discussion, but again, done in the right spirit, this process can be highly beneficial in clarifying issues and establishing priorities. The groups must be counseled that disappointment is one of the risks they face when investing their work, time and energy into unassigned problems/projects. Management, on the other hand, must be counseled to be sensitive to the efforts of the groups and avoid appearing arbitrary when dealing with the ideas proposed.

Having many groups working to improve the organization is both a wonderful social mechanism and an invaluable asset to the organization. While these are the most important advantages of having a network of OD groups, there are others. For example, the network provides many channels of communication which can be very valuable. Management can send messages to the groups via the current chairperson which is an alternative to the regular chain of command. Similarly, the group can pass information upward without being blocked or filtered by the various levels of management. Openness is promoted, and while this can be politically risky for some individuals, it can be extremely helpful when developing an organization to achieve both maximum productivity and high morale.

Another advantage of the network is that it tends to foster better communications across the pyramid, not just up and down. This is accomplished through a reporting system that in brief, involves joint group meetings, the exchanging of representatives between groups, and the formation of temporary groups using members of various permanent groups.

Still another advantage of the network is the ready mechanism it provides for resolving conflicts that may arise among the various groups. The procedures, processes and common jargon everyone uses helps them to deal rationally with abstract and emotional issues and helps to quickly surface and resolve misunderstandings and negotiate differences.

Designing the Network

There are six steps necessary to design and install your network of OD groups:

1. Stabilize the pyramid

2. Select the groups

3.   Train and develop the groups

4.   Set up the administrative/communication mechanism.

5.   Use the network to avoid and resolve conflicts.

6.   Make sure the power structure gives the network official and unofficial recognition and support.

Here are a few comments about each of these steps.

1.   Stabilize the pyramid.

Stabilizing the pyramid means to adopt a basic organization design which includes role assignments and reporting relationships. It is by no means necessary to have a perfectly planned or designed organization before you start training and developing groups, forming your network or using any of the other OD techniques discussed in earlier chapters. If it were, some organizations would never be ready.

For those organizations that have been traditionally remiss in adopting a basic design, forming groups is probably the best way to develop a sound structure. This can be accomplished by starting the group training and development with the most powerful group in the organization. This should be the executive committee made up of the chief executive officer and those reporting to him. The problem solving and project planning procedures and group processes blend beautifully with long range planning, manpower planning, organization design, executive compensation programs, and organization mission setting. Developing the executive committee provides the wherewithal to focus on the needs for identifying and prioritizing all the human resource development needs of the organization. So while the organization pyramid doesn't have to be perfectly fitted with each element receiving perfect support from below and guidance from the top, it does help if the structure is sufficiently stable so that people may leave or be reassigned, but the positions will have relative permanence. This leads to taking the next step toward developing your network.

2.   Select the groups.

Usually management is best equipped to determine the number, makeup, and general mission of the various permanent groups, whether they are sibling groups or special function groups. For this reason it is usually best to train and develop the management groups first, starting at the top of the pyramid and working downward. Minor variations in the progression is not a serious problem. Once a manager experiences the group development process, sees the immediate benefits and gains an appreciation for the long range potential benefits, he/she is eager to have his/her people similarly trained. The answer to the question of which special groups should become part of the network is highly dependent on the nature of the organization. There is no way I can generalize here about what functions they should deal with.

The temporary groups are similarly difficult to categorize for all organizations. The Task Team concept, however, is gaining rapid acceptance in major organizations. In some organizations it seems to be blurring the structure of the pyramid. Some team members in organizations that have widely accepted the concept report to their specific leader or boss only in the administrative sense. They operate as members of one or more task teams in a leader, follower or peer capacity. They work almost exclusively with other task team members and deal with the person they report to only for new assignments, compensation matters and administrative details having to do with insurance, personnel policies and the like.

The job of these individuals can truly be described as a task team member. Task team members may also belong to an OD specialty group as well. That is, he/she may work as an engineer on one or more task teams and also be on the safety committee, the plant picnic committee, and the president's advisory group for ecological matters, any of which may be relatively permanent or short lived. In organizations where the team or group membership concept is practiced, people often think of themselves as having two bosses, as in a matrix organization. This organization structural form is sometimes accepted with misgivings. It seems to me that most of the ill feelings stem from the prejudice people have against serving two masters because of the biblical injunction to that effect. Other writers on the subject point out that most of us, as children, were raised by two parents, both of whom had power over us. Therefore having two bosses is not a difficult concept nor an insurmountable problem if the spirit of the organization is open and one-on-one negotiation is possible. It's true no man can serve two masters in a master/slave relationship, but I believe it is possible in modern work organizations for a person to report to two different people on different matters.

Here are some reports of organizations that use groups or teams:

Packaging Division, Union Carbide Corporation: Use of problem solving teams raised 1974 production rates over 1/3...without having to add to the work force. Direct labor unit costs dropped significantly.

"Personnel Journal," August, 1975

Litton Microwave Cooking Division, Litton Industries: Use of task teams was a significant factor in the division's growth from $13 million to $130 million. During the same 5 year period, unit production increased from 125 units per day to over 3,000 units per day; profits increased 75% annually.

"Harvard Business Review," March–April, 1977

Fenton Art Glass Co.: Teams completed over 30 money saving projects in 18 months. One quality improvement project saves nearly $10,000 per year. Use of teams improved sharing of technical knowledge and skills among workers, significant reduction in grievances.

State of New Jersey, Department of Labor and Industry: Initial projects of pilot groups included: $3,600 savings by eliminating need for overtime in payroll section; reduced material waste and production time in making microfiche copies, saving $3,000 per year; usual six day delay in preparing major reports was eliminated while improving accuracy by 75%; and a clerical department established a workflow quality checkpoint system which reduced errors and saved about 30 man-hours per week.

Ortho-Pharmaceutical Corporation: A management team developed a new managerial development program which saved $50,000 per year by reducing turnover; revised craft training programs saving $80,000 in training costs. "First year return on task team training investment was 10 to 1."

"Personnel Journal," April, 1975

General Foods: Use of teams at Topeka, Kansas plant resulted in unit costs 5% lower than any other plant (saving about $1 million per year); turnover of only 8%; 3 years and eight months before its first lost-time accident.

"Business Week," March 28, 1977

Unnamed automotive division of a large multiplant, multidivisional corporation: Significantly improved quality of output; significant improvement in profit through reduced waste and fewer reworks. More positive attitudes among workers; more positive perception of management.

"Administrative Science Quarterly," June, 1975

Heritage Federal Savings and Loan Association: Team approach resulted in growth of assets from $200 million to $275 million in 18 months: use of team management resulted in a "marked increase of leadership ability in individual board members....leading to greater depth in managerial talent."

"FHLBB Journal," January, 1977

U.S. Army Communications Command and Subordinate Commands: Team building resulted in more effective organization, improved interpersonal skills, increased trust, improved ability to resolve conflicts.

Gould, Inc., Mack Truck, Inc. G.E., The Bendix Corporation, TRW, Inc., Abbott Laboratories, D.E.C., Dictaphone Corporation, Calgon Corporation: Representatives of these companies shared their common experiences in which a team approach was essential for successful implementation of their materials management programs.

"Purchasing," January, 1977

Pullman, Car Works No. 1: Doubled productivity, improved morale among 1st line supervisors, union complaints are down; many more grievances that might have been lodged are settled quickly by foremen and general managers.

"Production Engineering," January, 1977

<u>Maritime Tel & Tel</u> in Halifax, Nova Scotia increased their productivity by 75% and cut their absenteeism and turnover rate in half without any additional hiring or increasing their work space. This was accomplished by employees serving as interviewers to find out what was hindering their productivity. Teams of employees devised solutions to the problems. The astounding results were recorded six months after the new solutions were implemented.

"Personnel Journal," April, 1979

3.   <u>Train and develop the groups.</u>

Since this has been covered extensively in Chapter 7 there is no need for further detail here. But perhaps it should be emphasized that while the general nature of the procedures and processes that each group is trained to use will be generally the same, the exercises and activities and the amount of time they take will vary from group to group. In some cases a brief seminar will launch the group with no trouble. Other groups, particularly those composed of first line blue collar workers who may be unfamiliar with seminar work, may require several short meetings on location where the work is done. Such groups usually work on performance or productivity improvement projects.

It is safe to assume that all members can learn the basic techniques of participative problem solving and interpersonal communications. It is also safe to assume that most people will be interested in the success of their groups and their organization. Your experiences and your observations of current conditions may make this difficult for you to believe. You'll need a little faith and recognition of the fact that we are an extremely versatile species. How we behave is largely dependent on the situation we find ourselves in. If you change the environment you influence the behavior of the people. Conversely, if you can change the people you can change the environment. That's what the Orgeist and OD is all about.

4.   <u>Set up the administration and communication sys-
     tem.</u>

The time and paper work involved in setting up and
maintaining the network can be very simple and relatively undemanding. When a group is first formed, the basic
details are reported to everyone up the chain of
command in its segment of the pyramid. This report is
usually limited to the name of the group, the members,
its current mission statement, when and where it expects
to meet, and the problems, opportunities and/or projects
the group expects to work on in the foreseeable future.
You can request any other details that may be useful to
your own organization structure. A copy of this basic
data should be kept in a central file of OD groups and
made accessible to everyone who may use the information for the good of the organization.

There is no real need to keep minutes, yet many
groups feel more comfortable having them, at least at
first. More useful is the assignment list that comes out
of every group meeting. At the end of each session the
members of the group report to the others what they are
going to do and when they plan to do it as a result of the
meeting. This serves as an excellent source of feedback
for the group itself. Misconceptions can be cleared up
and people can be committed or contracted to do certain
things as their part of the group effort. The assignments
can be typed up and given to all group members plus the
interested members of management right up to the chief
executive officer if appropriate. Since most groups tend
to meet at least monthly, everyone concerned can watch
the group's progress.

A third report may be desirable. This one only
covers the problems/projects the group is working on and
those it hopes to work on in the near future. This report
can be combined with those from all other groups and
published on a periodic basis. The many advantages to
such a system include: avoiding duplication of effort,
sharing of valuable data and experiences, obtaining
offers of help, and exposure of individual members to

others in the organization both for ego satisfaction and to showcase unusual talents. Some network organizations use the house organ to publicize the work of the OD groups, while others circulate a separate newsletter to key people.

5.   Use the network to avoid and resolve conflicts.

Once your basic groups have been trained and developed and are operating within the network, the members are prepared to deal with conflict between groups. The Orgeist is already at work. People know about conflict and about interpersonal and intergroup processes and they know there is a technology for dealing with them. Ideally, part of the group's development training will include preparation for intergroup work.

Your groups should be trained to identify the other groups that are important to them and the ones they are in present or potential conflict with. Further, they should be trained how to approach the other group for an intergroup development effort. This training includes coverage of the traditional win/lose type of thinking that characterizes most people and groups in conflict situations. These are situations, of course, where one party emerges the victor and the other the loser. But in most cases victory is only in the eyes of the beholder. This is particularly true when the conflict is between parties who somehow depend upon one another. Today's winner is tomorrow's loser which means that any win/lose situation is really a lose/lose situation. Win/win situations are where both parties are winners and feel that the conflict must be settled in that way or it has really not been settled at all.

Many intergroup conflicts can be avoided by each group's sensitivity to the territories and concerns of other groups. This can be done in a systematic way so that the group can anticipate which forces in the organization are likely to support or oppose its actions. Groups can also avoid conflict through more expert "selling" of their ideas to other groups and persons.

Selling here refers to carefully developing a proposal tailored to specific interest groups and presenting it in a way that will not arouse opposition for anything other than the actual merits of what is being presented.

Should a real conflict arise between groups and be considered as significantly detrimental to the short or long term interest of the organization or the members, either group should take steps toward initiating a confrontation meeting. This type of meeting is intended to surface all issues between two groups in a manner that promotes fair and objective handling of the differences. It is the Orgeist doing its finest work and it is a joy to see it develop.

The procedure for the meeting is relatively simple, but should be facilitated by a consultant if either group has not been through the procedure at least once. Here are the steps:

1. Consultant addresses both groups jointly and explains the objectives and the procedure to everyone's satisfaction.

2. Groups go into separate rooms and develop a list of all the favorable things they know and feel about the other group.

3. Groups meet jointly and read and explain what they have listed---no discussion other than answering questions of clarification.

4. Groups work in separate rooms and develop lists of things that the other group does that have a negative impact on them.

5. Groups meet together and read and explain lists---again no discussion or arguments, just questions of clarification and the offering of information that anyone feels might be helpful to both groups.

6. Groups work separately on what they plan to do, being as specific as possible, to stop doing those things that are hurting the other group and start doing things to help them.

7. Groups meet together and take turns explaining what they plan to do to help each other more and hurt each other less. Suggestions on refinements and adjustments are allowed. The entire group may decide to work on certain problems, and/or sub-groupings or representatives of both groups may be appointed to work on specific problems.

8. A followup meeting date and other check-points are agreed to before adjournment.

Intergroup conflict resolution meetings such as this usually require a minimum of one day and possibly two or more just to get started. There is no way to predict the need for future meetings.

6. Support the network.

A well trained and developed network of OD groups with a simple administrative system should be virtually trouble free. The whole idea is to provide the opportunity for more people to be self directing in looking for ways to serve the organization, and the network is a very practical means to that end. However, networks do need the support of the power structure. The easiest way to undercut the network's effectiveness is to ignore it. Another way is to treat it like an interesting experiment in organization behavior. If you do, your people will judge it similarly and will interpret the reasoning behind the network as another attempt to make people feel good without really changing. Many training and human relations programs are used in this way. Only the naive really believe them to be anything other than a vain hope on management's part to deal with the involvement need without changing either themselves or their method of operation.

Other ways to render the network ineffectual is to ignore or denigrate the work of the groups, ignore their proposals, suggest that the groups don't have sufficient information, and by implication, the ability and experience necessary to deal with certain matters. If you want the network to succeed you must do everything in your power to make it succeed. You will have to read as many of the reports as you can. Send reaction notes and memos with useful ideas and sources of information. Interact with each group. Better yet, invite representative group members of an entire group to meet with or sit in on a meeting of the executive group. It would also help to attend as many group meetings as possible. Once trained and developed, the groups should be able to function normally even with very powerful figures present. Concerned and supportive attention to the group and to the people in them is and will always be the best motivation technique at the disposal of the prince(ss). Great generals, as mentioned earlier, walk among their troops despite the best staffed organization structure. Few people outgrow their need for stroking from powerful figures.

The OD Team

A team of organization members aided by an internal or external consultant can be an excellent aid to help sustain the network. This was mentioned earlier in Chapter 5. A special-permanent group composed of members representing a cross section of the entire organization and selected for their interest in OD efforts is ideal. Future internal consultants might spring from this group.

The OD team should be charged with constantly monitoring the network, providing reinforcement when needed and looking for ways to renew the organization through positive change. The formation of such a group usually requires special training and development efforts. Once in operation, the team should also have a special relationship with the most powerful people in the organization. Membership in this group should change, but at a relatively slow pace.

Costs

The development of such a network is a time consuming and expensive enterprise when you consider the hours lost from other work, the consultant fees, materials, meeting rooms, travel and meal costs and the sundry other expenses involved. When completed, and even before, the network should become a valuable organization asset and as such, should return to the organization more than it costs to develop and maintain. In most cases the return will be very difficult to measure and like a great number of other expenses spent on human resources development, must be made solely on faith.   If, however, you are willing to devote the additional time and energy necessary, it is possible to arrive at fairly accurate cost and return on investment figures for the work of the various groups and even the entire network.

With new groups this is relatively easy. Part of the training and development should be devoted to identifying, prioritizing and solving a problem or planning a project that is sensible for them to deal with. The costs and the potential savings or gain can be worked out during the training and development session. As time goes on and the group works on a variety of problems and projects, sometimes two or more simultaneously, it may be more difficult. However, the costs for the meetings which are usually held on the premises with no travel or subsistance can be easily absorbed.

Results

What can you expect in addition to more expenses, more problems solved, more projects completed, and more of your human resources used more efficiently? You can expect gains in productivity. To get all this involvement without better organization performance would be a terrible waste for a work organization. If the prime purpose or mission of the organization is to provide certain benefits to the members, such as in a social club, this concept would still apply. Why? Because the reason for people forming an organization is to produce things, services or events. Should the time come when the members feel their own interests come before the organization's, there will be no reason to have an organization. More of whatever you organized for can be obtained if more of your people want to help you achieve it.

On the more mundane side, the typical work organization that adopts OD concepts and utilizes OD technology such as group development and networks of OD groups can expect more meetings to take place. Highly structured organizations that consider and use people more like machines than thinking heads will find this abhorrent and well they should. Nobody said an organization must be participative in full or even in part. But consider that in even highly routinized production organizations, participative techniques have been successfully used. At the lowest levels in the organization, workers can participate in meetings that are devoted to performance improvement through behavior modification. This technique was briefly described in Chapter 5. Behavior modification means that people's behavior can be shaped depending on how they are rewarded or ignored. Done unilaterally, this approach is in direct opposition to the spirit of OD. For example, turning up the lights or the heat to influence work behavior is manipulative, and manipulation can influence people to work. We are all manipulative at times and are at other times manipulated. Should the cost to the individual be low, or in a good cause, or if we believe that manipulation is the role of management, we forgive those who use it. But most people know when they are being manipulated and they usually resent it. The negative feelings and actions it eventually leads to negates the temporary increase in production that may come from it.

There is a compromise that can be used, one that both rewards desired behavior and one that is not unilaterally manipulative. I call it <u>performance improvement through participative behavior modification.</u> The technique is a three step effort. First, teach first line workers, for example, about the principles of behavior modification. Show them through exercises and activities, as well as case examples, how we all tend to do those things that we perceive will be rewarded, particularly if the rewards immediately follow the desired behavior.

The next step is to make sure the workers identify with the success of their group and the organization. They must want to succeed and willingly participate in ways to make it more successful. The next step is to enlist the help of the group in identifying the performance they want to improve and the rewards that would encourage them to seek the improvements. These may have to be negotiated if large expenditures are involved, but once all concerned agree, it is a matter of keeping score and distributing the rewards. In short, the game is more fun to play if you have a voice in making up the rules and in making sure they are administered fairly.

You can also expect the network to precipitate a great deal more open discussion and even confrontation about organization issues. You may feel these issues are the sole province of yours and other organization leaders, but try to accept it as the price of objective cooperation. With the right skills you won't find this a threatening situation. When all parties are properly trained to deal with conflict openly, it can and should be welcomed.

There will also be a dramatic increase in the number and quality of information exchanges among organization members. Contacts made in and between groups facilitates easy access to other organization members, peer and non-peer alike.

You will also find a transfer of problem solving and creative skills to individual work. The procedures recommended for group problem solving can easily be adapted to individual work on a great variety of tasks and assignments.

If this all sounds too good to be true, maybe it is. Remember, you are the most important person in your segment of the organization. Only you can make it happen and to quote a currently popular saying, "If you think you can or you think you can't, you're right."

You will find a number of resource items that you can use to set up and run your network described in Chapter 11. ˙the next chapter explains how to start the change process---to more productive participation---in your organization.

CHAPTER 9

STARTING AND SUSTAINING THE CHANGE PROCESS ---
IN GOOD TIMES AND BAD

This chapter is the call to action. By now you no doubt have many ideas, hopes, and doubts about your willingness and ability to promote participativeness along the lines I have been suggesting. You will have to get your "head on straight" as the expression goes. You will have to decide if you have the power, the opportunity, the personal inclination, the knowledge, and skills that it will take to develop yourself, your people, their relationships, your groups, your network of groups, plus all the spin-off activities that will result in the new Orgeist that will be evidenced throughout your organization.

My advice is to give it a try despite any doubts. Is this because I'm so convinced that the techniques I've described will work in any organization or segment of it? The answer is --- no, I am not. There is no technique or system that can be designed so well that it will succeed without the commitment of the people, particularly the most powerful person(s). I confidently say: go ahead --- give it a try, because what I am suggesting can be tried cautiously, one step at a time. Certainly you can expect opposition, because most changes bring opposition. You need not openly commit yourself to the total system in any given time period. You can proceed when you are ready and at a pace acceptable to your people. Think of your OD efforts as akin to planting a seed and nurturing its growth rather than as designing and building a mechanical system that you will impose on an unsuspecting and unwilling people.

The ancient Chinese saying, "The longest journey starts with the first step," applies beautifully to this type of undertaking. Perhaps you have already taken some steps toward sensible participativeness already. If I know my readers, I suspect that you are at heart a participative type, either by conscious choice or by natural inclination, or both, and are looking for how-to advice and resources. If so, this book will meet a part of your need.

On the other hand, you may be looking for ways to react to a very bad current situation. If you are experiencing some form of internal conflict that is sapping or misdirecting the energies of your people, the start-up of your OD efforts may have to take a different track.

In this chapter I will offer both a general strategy for promoting more productive participativeness in the relatively sound and stable organization, and techniques for turning bad situations around.

The general strategy for either stable or threatened situations is basically the same:

A.   Provide sufficient structure without threatening official or unofficial power bases.

B.   Surface and solve or resolve problems.

C.   Sustain the spirit by interpreting rules, policies, and practices and by setting a personal example that says you wish to share both power and responsibility for performance with everyone.

Strategy for Stable Situations

Here is the strategy that I recommend when the design and structure of the organization is fairly well established. Keep in mind that the steps are fairly complex and will overlap and contain many sub-steps.

1.   Develop yourself --- decide where you want to go as a participative leader, how you plan to get there, and most of all, why?

2.   Develop a relationship with a consultant, either an internal or external person.

3.   Develop your relationships with key persons, subordinates and others.

4.   Develop your primary group; for the typical chief executive officer this would probably be the executive committee.

5.   Develop other groups: permanent, specialist, temporary task or project teams, and an OD consultant team.

6.   Develop the network.

7.   Develop the dyadic or one-on-one relationships vital to the organization.

8.   Develop the individual members of your organization.

These steps have been covered in previous chapters and are presented in capsule form below:

1.   Develop yourself.

This refers to that part of self development that deals with participativeness. It involves a personal assessment of your work needs and style, both as you perceive them and as others perceive them. Please understand that you are bound to have feelings of ambiguity and that you will have to operate more in an organic than in a mechanical way; otherwise, you won't be dealing with true participativeness. Be willing to take risks; the obstacles are mostly in your mind and not inherent in your organization.

2.   Develop the client/consultant relationship.

This is a matter of learning to accept help for a certain portion of your work life. It is help based on mutual trust, respect, and growth and not expertise alone. While your consultant should have sufficient knowledge and expertise in his/her field keep in mind that human relations and organization development is a dynamic growing body of knowledge and no one should be considered as an ideal model to be copied. Together you can solve problems, plan projects and handle other challenges that lead to increased productivity.

3. Develop relationships with key individuals.

You would naturally want your most trusted aids and co-workers to be in tune with your thinking before promoting your ideas elsewhere in the organization. This will require a great deal of formal and informal talking about your relationship, your feelings about participativeness and how you can work together to bring it about in a sensible way to increase productivity. Don't expect all of your key people to come along at the same pace. Immediate acceptance and compliance is as much a danger signal as rejection and avoidance. Try to start with a success, a relationship that you feel has a lot of natural things going for it. You want objective cooperation, a relationship of friends who want to cooperate but who feel free to disagree and can and will explain why. Then work on the more "challenging" relationships.

4. Develop your primary group.

This is a natural next step but it could possibly be done concurrently with the previous step or even before. If the relationships are already where you want them, you could concentrate on the skills of working together on problems or projects. You might then go right into the training and development of your primary group. If you are the CEO, this would be your executive committee or whatever you choose to call the group. You'll want to improve all the interpersonal relationships within the group, broaden everyone's sense of responsibility for the entire organization, and improve their group skills. At lower levels in the organization the same general objectives will apply to group development effort but will naturally concentrate on the problems/projects that make sense for a particular group to be working on, whether they are assigned by management or selected by the group.

5.   Develop other groups.

Your primary group should have a strong voice on what the make-up of the various pyramid, special, and temporary groups should be. They'll no doubt want a voice in the scheduling of the training and development of the groups and what kind of problems or projects they work on. They will be needed to support the groups in their efforts and recognize their results. The materials you can use to help you train and develop your groups are described in Chapter 11.

6.   Develop the network.

This is a relatively mechanical procedure and can be done simultaneously as the groups are developed. Part of the training and development sessions should include how to report efforts and results up the pyramid and across it. After the mechanics of the system have been set up, your network development efforts should be a matter of interacting with the various groups both alone and with your primary group. It will also mean encouraging the various groups to interact when appropriate either through joint meetings, jointly staffed subgroups and through the exchange of representatives.

7.   Develop the dyadic or one-on-one relationships that are vital to your organization's success.

This is a matter of helping your people use the same tools, techniques and strategies that you used with your immediate subordinates and others close and important to you in the organization. Some of this can be done while the groups are being developed and through special training programs aimed directly at such relationships, or on an "as needed" basis. Materials you can use to aid this effort are described in chapter 11. For those who have internal consultancy responsibilities, you will want to consider the materials described for that purpose. They are designed to help develop the relationship between you and your OD consultant but apply to other types of consultants and their relationships with users of their services as well.

8. Develop the individual members of your organization.

This is the last step in the general strategy I recommend. I'm referring in particular to the development of individual members as participants in solving the problems and realizing the opportunities that are inherent in your organization. Your people will, just as you did, have to get their heads on straight on this whole issue of participation. All won't readily accept the responsibilities that go with the opportunity. They'll develop at different paces. The development of the individuals along these lines starts with their participating in the group development efforts but may require reinforcement from time to time in the form of special training programs, group work and personal encouragement from you. It always comes back to you. The materials that are useful for helping your people develop as participating elements in your organization are the same ones that are helpful for you. They are described in Chapter 11.

Strategy for Unstable Situations

Now let's talk about starting your OD efforts under less than optimal conditions. Begin by understanding that it is better to start during relatively stable times. Law and order are necessary to freedom. The functions of participation are more difficult to start and sustain during times of confusion, conflict and disorder.

However, waiting for a modicum of peace and stability may be never ending. Some Machiavellians may even perpetuate instability to provide an excuse for "over control." If your organization has a long history of instability with all its attendant counter-productive elements, stop waiting. You have nothing to lose from a performance viewpoint. You may have something to lose from a personal one and if that is your prime concern, let Machiavelli be your guide and shelve this book.

When the barbarians are at the gates it is no time, because there is no time, to seek consensus on defense strategy. This is why the traditional pyramid structure should be preserved and respected. Because the defense is complex and every member's brain as well as brawn will be needed to prepare for a siege, participation is essential.

There is no way for me to anticipate all the possible emergencies and problems that will beset those who read this book. Comparatively few of you, I'm sure, will be called upon to lead under dangerous conditions. Most, I suspect, will be managers and executives in work organizations. And, while it's not inconceivable that you will have to take command in situations that call for quick decisive action, most often your problems in the organization will announce themselves in less dramatic ways.

The signs of trouble are well known to experienced managers: poor quality work, low production figures, increased absenteeism, tardiness, pilferage, grievances, walkouts, and wildcat strikes. Equally significant as problem indicators but perhaps more difficult to measure are such things as accidents, squabbles, sabotage, writing on washroom walls, negative behavioral norms, and unofficial groups that are less than friendly with other unofficial groups.

Naturally, the sooner organizational problems can be identified and dealt with the better. That's why it is so important to have an "open" climate where everyone can immediately call attention to and deal with problems they sense are brewing in the organization. But that's the ideal and seldom the real world. So let's talk about the in-between stage: the situations that could be improved but are not so desperate that the battle lines are drawn and all out war is about to begin.

A large percentage of the cases of organizational fragmentation or at least the most dramatic and best publicized are labor-management situations: the union is organizing or asking for things management doesn't want to give, or vice versa.

Union and non-union, by the way, are not the determinants of fragmentation and cooperation. Union-free industrial organizations can have great conflicts between first line workers and management. There may not be strikes or walkouts but the cost to the organization in terms of "heel dragging" and other counterproductive activities can be as costly as a strike.

Conversely, I have seen union shops that were virtually model climates of openness, trust, cooperation, and were highly productive. Everybody was concerned for the organization's success and was involved in identifying and dealing with the organization's problems and opportunities.

The union is just another power base for certain official and unofficial leaders. Therefore it must be dealt with as a power base. This means involving those with power in the responsibility taking, the problem solving and decision making. It also means surfacing the concerns of all involved and deciding on courses of action that meet the needs of the powerful.

Few organization leaders ever find it advantageous to invite the union in. Nor do they ask for more government regulators or consumer groups to evaluate their work. Such power bases would have to be contended with from that point on and they tend to restrict the power of management. They also impose more structure which can be detrimental if flexibility is necessary for the organization to meet its goals. Whether the goals themselves are good or bad is beyond the scope of this book.

The point I wish to make is this. Once a power
base has been established through a union or any other
means, it should be more than accepted. It should be
accepted and worked with. The adversary relationship is
almost always a negative element within the organization. Thinking along adversary lines is an inherent part
of our common cultural makeup. We think about them,
we take pride in them, we institutionalize them in our
legal and judicial system. Injecting legalistic concepts,
techniques and procedures into labor relations usually
does more harm than good. Organizations need climates
of good will and trust, not just surface calm based on a
myriad of rules to reach their full potential.

The traditional and usually ineffective way to deal
with conflict-ridden organizations when those in power
sincerely wanted to make peace with all power bases is
to conduct an attitude survey. These are usually lengthy
questionnaires covering all aspects of organization life.
The results are given to management which theoretically
takes corrective action. Sometimes the results are
openly shared with everyone and an action plan is
announced.

Another, more traditional response to seriously
fragmented organizations is to replace one or more
powerful persons. In many cases this is what is needed,
and in many more it can be avoided if the powerful
people can be helped to surface, confront and deal with
the issues that are dividing the organization.

I prefer very simple questionnaires that ask about
what organization performance factors need improving.
If possible, it is better to have people complete them in
small groups, tabulate the results as quickly as possible,
and give the information back to the groups for more
discussion. What this system lacks in scientific elegance
it makes up in opening meaningful dialogues on current
issues.

There are two other techniques for responding to
conflict situations and initiating OD efforts in less than

ideal organizational circumstances. The first is usually called Problem Sensing or Concern meetings and the other is a meeting format that can be described as "Listening and Helping" or "Fishbowl" meetings.

Concern Meetings

Concern meetings are not used to solve problems but to:

1. Identify the internal problems with people, processes and procedures.

2. Let everyone know that the powerful are aware that things are not right and are taking steps to do something about it.

These meetings can have a wide variety of formats, makeups and agendas depending on the situation. Sometimes they are conducted by an outside consultant who assures everyone of his/her objectivity and pledges absolute confidentiality. The consultant simply asks people what they feel is wrong about the organization and lists them on a chart page. He/she then asks those in the meeting to correct or refine what has been written if necessary. When all concerns have been recorded, an attempt may be made to combine the concerns under various headings. The consultant then takes the charts to management and explains as necessary and helps management plan a reaction to the concerns. The same thing can be accomplished by one or more consultants interviewing everyone concerned but this is time consuming, expensive and non-confrontive.

I prefer not to follow the last procedure described because it accentuates a "we-they" feeling. However, it may be necessary in organizations where mistrust is rampant. It is better to have the most powerful person conduct the meeting. I also suggest that before the meeting, participants be invited to register their concerns. They are prepared by the leader or a consultant by being told the ground rules:

1.   This is not a "gripe" session. If you are angry now, let's wait until we can talk coolly.

2.   Register concerns about the functioning of the organization but don't attack personalities.

3.   Candor, openness, directness is welcomed and encouraged. You can also tell why you are hampered in your work and what you think needs doing in general terms, but we are not here today to solve problems or debate solutions---just identify problems and get a feeling of the extent people are concerned about them.

Many variations are possible. For example, larger groups can be divided into smaller ones of six to ten and chaired by someone elected by the group to report out. Another variation would be to have the meeting limited to representatives of various groups in the organization. Regardless of the variations, it is important that the powerful really listen, treat the concerns seriously and immediately set a date for a followup meeting where the group can be sounded out again and management can report on what has been done thus far.

Listen/Help (Fishbowl)

The second technique I have used with great success is the Listen/Help or "Fishbowl" format. This technique can be used to resolve conflicts between two small groups or many large groups. I once worked with a client organization that was experiencing a considerable amount of conflict between those in the field sales organization and various production and support units. In addition, the various sales units communicated very little with each other.

The problem seen by sales people was that the largely commissioned sales organization was selling more than could be produced. Also, the slowness of delivery was considered to be due to incompetence. Those in non-sales roles believed them and felt guilty about it and often over-compensated by going to extremes to expedite orders in any way they could, regardless of standard procedures. Many resented the practices and attitudes of those in sales.

A national sales meeting was called but instead of the usual hoopla and forced positive thinking, an attitude of adult concern for everyone's problems was manifested. The meeting was preceded by "Need for Help" questionnaires to save time and gave management a running start on the more pressing problems. Also, the field sales managers were involved in group development efforts along with top sales management before the national sales meeting, so much was done to set the tone for "Confrontation without Conflict" and to prepare people to think about their relationships and their mutual dependence.

The Listen/Help Fishbowl session took up a great deal of the first two days of the meeting. They worked like this. Several meeting rooms were used at the same time. Each room was under the direction of an internal consultant who played the role of facilitator. The facilitator welcomed all, explained the objectives and format and kept time. He also intervened when necessary to keep things running as planned. Those not wishing to abide by the ground rules were given permission to leave before the meeting began. None did.

Smaller meeting rooms were assigned to specific "host" groups that sales interacted with: accounting, pricing, production, quality control, engineering, and so forth. Representatives from each sales office were assigned to each room and were told to come prepared with lists of compliments and complaints collected from their sales office for the host group. Each host group also prepared by collecting samples of productive and counterproductive behaviors they observed in salespeople. No names or locations were identified.

The fishbowl name comes from the seating arrangement. Members of the host group sat in a circle, around a table and simply discussed, under the direction of a chairperson, positive experiences they had with salespeople in the past, just as though they were alone in the room. The salespeople sat all around the group seated at the table---"theatre in the round" style. (The salespeople, or whoever sits in the outer ring around the fishbowl, are not permitted to speak or even ask questions, just listen.) After 15 to 30 minutes of listening, the sales group or representative members assumed their place in the fishbowl and, using their notes, engaged in a general conversation about their positive experiences with the host group.

The process is then repeated. The host group again sits in the fishbowl but this time they discuss their negative experiences with the salespeople, occasionally mentioning what they would like to see salespeople do. Again, the observing sales group is not permitted to interact with those in the fishbowl but they are encouraged to listen and take notes.

Finally, the salespeople sit in the fishbowl and discuss their negative experiences while the host group observes and takes notes. The facilitator then instructs both groups to meet separately and make preliminary plans on what they will start or stop doing to help the other group. The group spokesmen will report out during the last session of the national sales meeting.

The groups meet again and as often as necessary to formulate their plans to further help the other group. This may take several weeks, and in the case just described, reports were exchanged, discussed and further reports issued. If the groups are not scattered across the country, the groups could meet and negotiate in person.

In the case described, the groups were based on function in the organization because this is where the conflicts centered. The results were dramatic; many lines of communication opened up, relationships were strengthened and many problems solved.

The technique also works with non-functional groups as well. The grouping could be various levels of management, people at different facilities or locations, or even different informal groupings---along racial, sex, ethnic, professional, age, or any other lines.

The variations can be infinite but remember the basic intent is to surface and solve problems that make people feel bad and adversely affect performance or production. This is what almost everybody concerned wants most of the time, so find a way to do it. Do it without threatening anyone and by letting the basic good will and common sense most people have take over.

You probably won't be able to change your organization alone. You'll need helpers---internal and external consultants. The next chapter deals with how you can work with them.

CHAPTER 10

WORKING WITH INTERNAL AND
EXTERNAL CONSULTANTS

To put the use of consultants in proper perspective, let's first look at the "ideal" participative organization in terms of the values and concepts described in this book. Our ideal organization is one that makes the most of its opportunities in the world by using its resources in the most efficient and effective way while it serves the interests of owners, members, clients or customers, and society in the best possible way.

Internally, the organization is in a constant state of planned and participative change as it adapts to the restraints it encounters and opportunities that become available. Everyone relates well to others, all communicate clearly, solve problems and complete projects objectively and successfully. People take appropriate risks and live in an open climate of trust where their own potential for growth is fully realized.

Experienced people know that this ideal will likely never come to pass without divine intervention. We can, however, accept the ideal and use it as a general target. It can help us make decisions in everyday situations.

The ideal has a better chance of being realized, or at least more of it can be realized, if there is some structural support for the desired situation. That in a way is what the development of dyadic relationships, groups, and networks is all about.

The mechanism that will probably prove to be most effective in supporting the Orgeist is the OD consultant group (which was mentioned in Chapter 8). Ideally, this is a group of organization members selected for their interest in OD activities and their natural talents as facilitators. This group's members can work both individually and collectively on OD type problems they identify or those assigned by management. All levels of management and fields of endeavor should be represented and the group should have a very special relationship with the powerful persons in the organization. While the membership of the OD consultant group may change, the group and its mission should forever be a part of the organization.

It is very difficult, and in most cases impossible, for the OD consulting group to become fully functional on its own, just as it is for the formal leadership of the organization to start and sustain the participative process on its own. This is why the use of outside consultants will be the most direct and cost effective way to initiate your OD efforts.

The term "consultant" is one that is used to identify so many different persons and roles that it has become useless without relating it to very specific situations. This should not be an excuse to denigrate the term or the persons labeled as such. After all, there are many distinct types of psychologists and any one type may be almost totally ignorant of the problems and practices of another type, yet we use the title for all of them.

Naturally, in this book consultant refers to Organization Development consultants who may also be referred to as practitioners, specialists, facilitators or process consultants. Like other professionals they come from different backgrounds, training, and expertise, and they practice in the framework of various schools of thought within the profession. While there are organizations that are attempting to accredit and control the use of the title and the practice of Organization Development, the field is currently open to anyone who decides to adopt the profession. Of course, there is no assurance that official accreditation brings skill, expertise, moral righteousness or effectiveness, just as with any other profession.

I use the term consultant to refer to a person contracted to provide a certain expertise under the umbrella of a very special relationship with the prince(ss) or group of individuals to help bring about some mutually agreed upon change. It may be called a project or a problem solving attempt or simply a way of bringing a planned change into the organization. Indeed, some OD consultants prefer to be called change agents.

The purpose of this chapter is to help you become more aware of what an Organization Development consultant is and is not, select consultants who will be effective with your organization, learn how to work with your consultants, and encourage you to help everyone in your organization develop and use consulting skills.

First, a few words to impress upon you the importance of working with consultants. It is unfortunate but true that most people in our culture still feel that there is some sort of stigma attached to seeking help for personal and interpersonal problems. Similarly, some organization leaders feel it is a weakness to seek the help of consultants for people problems. Many will only seek and employ such help when it can be purchased or taken under the guise of some other heading. It is okay to use technicians or specialists because of lack of internal expertise or because of a heavy work load, but using an objective party for helping to integrate the organization's elements sounds too much like getting help for what the executive is supposed to do.

It is not necessary to be sick to get better. Those leaders who employ or contract with OD consultants are generally on the more secure and confident side. They recognize that seeking help is a sign of strength. They also recognize that OD is an emerging technology and one they can't be expected to have naturally acquired along with the mantle of leadership. The ranks of professional consultants have grown tremendously over the past few years and while some are, as the popular gag goes, "consultants only because they have not been gainfully employed for over six months," most are highly qualified specialists who sell their skills and energy on a project or retainer basis to a great variety of organizations. In addition, more and more internal specialists are being officially designated as consultants. Those who were formally considered staff specialists and whose role was to give specialized support to line managers as requested, now think of themselves as professionals with responsibilities to their own function, their profession, the entire organization, and themselves as well as to their clients. All interests must be respected and one is not to be served at the expense of another.

In your role as an organization prince(ss), the number of internal and external consultants you deal with and the extent you will spend your resources working with them, will be in proportion to your level in the organization. The great variety of complex fields necessary to make an organization successful, plus the need for objectivity, will mean that your future holds many hours of work with consultants. Learning how to best select them and work with them, and helping your people acquire consulting skills and developing these skills yourself, is of great importance to your own effectiveness as a participative prince(ss) and the success of your organization.

Every technical specialty has spawned legions of consultants, most of whom can more accurately be described as experts or specialists with sources of information and skills to apply to various problems recognized in the organization. Organization Development consultants cannot be technical specialists alone. True, there is already a great body of concepts, strategies, techniques, and specialized skills that OD consultants can draw upon. And, while the OD consultant is expected to use them and teach them to others, his/her real role is to help individuals and ultimately the whole organization to adopt and use the OD technology that will best help them change for the better.

Internal Consultants

Internal consultants are those who are part of the organization, on the payroll, and reporting to someone in the organization. External consultants are apart from the organization and working with the organization on a temporary basis.

Most large organizations have found that technical expertise can be hired more cheaply than contracted for. In some cases and for some fields, the larger organization employs an internal specialist and uses outside resources as well, such as law firms and advertising agencies. When it comes to OD, this practice has some very real advantages and disadvantages.

Internal OD consultants are generally considered to lack the same kind of objectivity that external ones have but this is not necessarily true. A member of an internal OD consulting group can be assigned to various divisions in the large organization and can assume an objective stance with that segment of the organization. The problem that may arise is that the individual or group client does not perceive the consultant as objective. If the consultant is viewed as an agent of top or central management or of a certain faction, his/her effectiveness is limited. This inherent limitation can be overcome and the trust level raised with time and effort.

The internal consultant may be less expensive if his/her services will be needed for a long period of time. They also are more likely to be familiar with the idiosyncrasies and structural makeup of the organization. The external consultant invariably must go through some sort of familiarization process with the client organization.

External Consultants

The external consultant's advantage in OD efforts is his/her objectivity. This can be compromised somewhat by the type of contract he/she has with the prince(ss) or the organization. The method of payment for consulting efforts can be on a retainer basis, project basis, daily fee, or results obtained basis. Most commonly the consultant works for a set daily fee for a certain number of days. Renewal of the contract for another period or project is usually predicated on performance, as judged by the person or group who engages him/her.

External consultants are particularly useful when dealing with the more powerful figures in the organization. As we have discussed earlier, the power issue is of great importance in organization development efforts. The internal consultant, particularly if he/she is several rungs down the management ladder, is severely handicapped when dealing with powerful people in the organization.

A combination of internal and external consultants can be very effective. Larger organizations can profitably use a permanent OD consulting group consisting of external and internal professionals. The smaller organizations can use a combination of external consultants and an internal group composed of individuals with an interest in and a proclivity for OD efforts who also hold other positions in the organization. These methods, however, assume a rather broad based and permanent acceptance of OD. In the earlier stages of OD efforts and in smaller organizations it is best to use an external consultant.

The Consultant's Role

The consultant, like every member of the organization, should be concerned with the overall problems and opportunities of the organization. He/she should be aware of how the interest groups --- the owners, top management, the customers or clients, and society at large all have a stake in the welfare of the organization and that the members are just one of the interest groups. However, the main focus of the OD consultant's efforts is directed at how the members interact in pursuit of the organization's goals. He/she must above all recognize that the concerns of the interest groups and the success of the organization are directly related to how members skillfully and objectively cooperate.

It is the responsibility of the consultant to become aware of all the forces that influence individual and organization behavior, then to help the client become aware of them and to discover ways to bring about the change that is desired. OD consultants use traditional tools and techniques for both diagnostic and intervention efforts. They use surveys, interviews, observation, consultation with individuals, and meetings with groups. However, they are more sensitive to the interaction of all the forces covered in the S x C x T x M = I/O P formula explained in Chapter 3. (Structure X Communications X Training X Motivation = Individual and/or Organization Performance.)

They are also highly aware that to help people change, they must start with the perceptions of the individuals involved. Helping people to understand how they see things and alternate ways of seeing them is essential to helping them make decisions about changing their behavior. This, more than anything, describes the OD consultant's role.

The Client/Consultant Relationship

OD consultants can be most effective when their client recognizes that he/she "owns" the organization's problems and opportunities. The consultant's role is that of a helping person and he/she should never assume the client's role. Their relationship must necessarily be one of mutual trust where each can be honest with the other without fear of being used. In short, the client/consultant contract should be based on both party's needs and expectations.

Very powerful people who achieved their status because of their high need for power, as noted in Chapter 4, may find it difficult to get their heads and hearts synchronized. They may want to be participative leaders and utilize the OD technology available to them, but find it difficult to do all the things that will enable their people to see them as supportive of participative practices. If so, the OD consultant has much work to do with the client before going on to the other vital relationships in the organization.

Power monopolizing leaders may consciously or unconsciously hinder the OD effort by doing one or more of the following:

-    Hiring a consultant to bring the blessings of participation to other parts of the organization but not those that he/she dominates

-    Expecting the consultant to play the role of the expert who will turn things around or straighten them out for a fee

-    Treating the consultant as a temporary employee who needs close supervision

-    Undercutting the consultant's efforts or otherwise competing with him/her to thwart change

-    Calling a halt to the OD effort at the first sign of resistance rather than recognizing the resistance to change is natural and a necessary stage of development

Figure 7 helps to illustrate the range of client/consultant relationships. It is the same model used to depict the more powerful/less powerful person relationship in Chapter 6. The lines representing each party cross to show how either party may dominate the other. At the left, the client is on top and the consultant at the extreme bottom of the model. This relationship would be like a traditional user of services and the one providing the service typical of most line officers and staff person relationships. At the other extreme we have the consultant serving as expert or guru to the student or as a doctor to a patient. Neither relationship is conducive to objective problem solving. The middle, where the lines cross to represent situations where the power issue has been negated, is best. Neither party dominates; BOTH objectively solve the problem together.

FIGURE 7

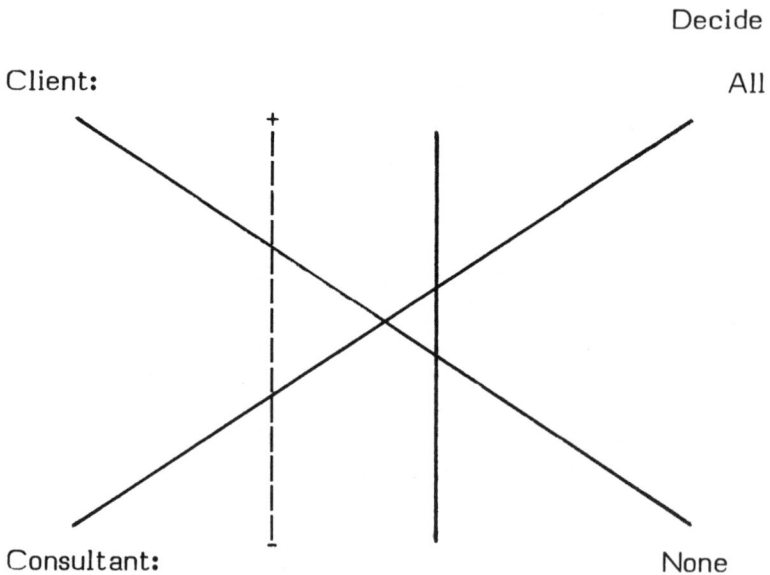

Decide

Client: All

Consultant: None

The person who completed this model indicates that he/she sees the present relationship (broken line) as one where the client is dominant and feels good about it (the + sign) and the consultant is not happy about it (the - sign). The perceiver believes the consultant should be slightly more in control of the decision making process at this time as indicated by where he/she placed a solid vertical line.

A cartoon I love to show those who seem not to value the great potential of consultants depicts a princely warrior stepping out of his field tent to lead his waiting troops who are armed with swords and spears. The prince's aide tries to direct his attention to a smug little man with a machine gun waiting to see the prince. The caption has the prince saying: "I don't have any time to see some crazy consultant - we've got a battle to fight!" You may feel supremely confident that you know about the OD technologies available and what it is all about. You may be certain that OD cannot be used to help you or your organization become more productive. You may have already harnessed the tremendous power of your human resources. But if you have not, don't turn your back on the idea of using the right consultant. He/she can help your organization become internally more cooperative so that it can successfully adapt in a changing world.

Selection of an OD Consultant

The selection of an OD consultant is no different than selecting any other professional helper. Most people rely on the referrals of others whose judgment they trust. You can start your selection process by contacting various professional associations or universities for names of OD consultants in your area. You can then screen them by reviewing their credentials, experiences, and references. This can be an arduous task. The number of people identifying themselves as OD consultants grows daily and membership in an organization or being on the staff of an institution is no indicator of expertise, let alone compatability.

As an experienced leader you no doubt have to exercise judgment regarding the abilities and compatability of others---employees, suppliers, and various types of consultants. Ultimately, you will have to rely on your personal judgment. The best indicator, aside from personal chemistry, is to see if the consultant seems willing and able to start with your perceptions, the way you see things, and then work on your relationship with him/her before launching into a full blown effort.

If the chemistry seems right from the start, commit to a short term effort and evaluate the experience openly with the consultant before deciding whether and how to go further. Once the trust level is high and the bond strong, committing to larger blocks of time and effort will give the effort stability and strength.

After I served my term as the founding chairperson of CODA---the Chicago Organization Development Association---I was asked to chair a committee to develop a code of ethics for our members, half of which are internal consultants and the other half external consultants. Here is the code that was adopted:

As a member of the Chicago Organization Development Association and as an OD practitioner, I believe in striving to:

1.   Maintain a stance of concerned objectivity in all relations with my clients, keeping in mind the confidence and trust they place in me and the power my professional background gives me to influence their welfare.

2.   Serve the interests of both client organization and those who are members of the organization but not serve one at the expense of the other.

3.   Help my clients understand and accept the ultimate responsibility for solving their own problems and realizing their own opportunities and never to allow my clients to become dependent on our continuing relationship.

4.   Help my clients reach meaningful and measurable objectives in the shortest possible time for the lowest possible cost.

5. Contribute to my professional development and the growth of the Organization Development profession by actively sharing research, ideas, and experiences with other practitioners.

6. Promote public awareness of OD and confidence in its practitioners, particularly the great promise it holds for helping individuals and organizations to be more successful.

My experience indicates that most practitioners accept and follow this code and the spirit it suggests. Most of us in the profession seem to have a strong need to help. We tend to be very analytical individuals of a rather independent nature. We enjoy being both part of an organization's effort while being apart from it. We like dealing with people with power and being, therefore, somewhat powerful ourselves. However, we know that our power lasts only as long as we are <u>perceived</u> to be serving the interests of others. We never become tenured, we can't expect to use the organization as a power base or an income source, or for any of the security and ego support functions for which most people belong to organizations. We can come in for a while, help, and leave, perhaps to come back on various related assignments or for new problems and opportunities that arise in the future. We enjoy our work and perhaps, like most professionals, we overrate our role and our technology, but we believe we have what is the best hope for the big problems of the world: productivity, personal growth, cooperation, and good feelings towards ourselves and others. Our faith in our profession is great, almost religious. However, our methods are far different than traditional religious ones. We try to influence thoughts and behaviors not by preaching, laying down rules of behavior, nor by using guilt, rituals, majestic trappings, priestly or group pressures. Our methods rely on enlightened self interest, objectivity, cooperation, measurable progress, and respect for all persons and organizations. However, I can make no claim that what we or our clients do is necessarily moral. We can work with organizations whose ends are essentially immoral by your standards or another's. Morality is and always will be an issue that every person will have to deal with individually.

As a prince(ss) with power in your pyramid, you will have many opportunities to work with internal and external consultants as well as play the consultant role yourself. When dealing with OD efforts, or when doing anything to help people interact more effectively, it helps if everyone understands and/or can assume the role of the consultant. It is the role of bringing the best out of a relationship of peers, power unequals, within groups, or between groups. It is everyone's job in the organization.

When every individual and group in the organization is linked to every other individual and group in a network of consulting relationships, you'll find the organization has been "developed". It can fully use its human resources to become maximally productive. Being a prince or princess in such an organization is a joy. May your reign be so blessed.

CHAPTER 11

RESOURCES YOU CAN USE TO PROMOTE PARTICIPATION AND IMPROVE PRODUCTIVITY

Unlike typical seminars and training programs, the materials used in OD efforts tend to play a secondary role. They are relatively unimportant. Multicolor printing, elaborate binders, or flashy audiovisual materials are fairly rare in activities associated with the development of relationships and groups. They should be.

Fancy packages are often empty. It's the results that count and not what looks good on the shelf. Most group development sessions use a variety of one or two page items to structure experiences, and a flip chart, felt markers and masking tape. Some consultants use no materials at all. I prefer very simple, easy to use and understand printed materials. Most of them were developed in response to specific challenges with client organizations by myself or my associates. Some were adapted from items used by other consultants.

My current resource file contains over one hundred items from which I select those that I believe will best help me when working with individuals, groups, and organization-wide problems.

My resource file is available to you. Those items that require it come with consultant guides that explain how and when to use the item. You'll find the Organization Development Consultant's Resources package a valuable, much used asset. The package is available through the publishers of this book. It can be used by either an experienced external consultant or a relatively inexperienced internal one that will help you to grow through the OD experience.

The package of materials is divided into six categories:

Series #100 --- for developing individuals

Series #200 --- for developing client/consultant relationships

Series #300 --- for developing one-on-one relationships

Series #400 --- for training and developing groups

Series #500 --- for developing a network of groups and intergroup relationships

Series #600 --- for developing organization diagnostic data

The entire set contains over 100 different items: instruments, exercises, planning devices, and consultant's guides. All are easy to understand and use and are applicable to any type of organization.

The purchase of the package of materials includes a license to duplicate and use the materials in your organization indefinitely. A copy of the license is on the following page.

The number of items in the package will probably increase and newer versions of certain items are likely to be developed as time goes on. Therefore, the specific items included are guaranteed for only one year from the date of publication of this book. A purchase order showing prices is included at the back of the book. If it is missing, current prices can be obtained from the publisher, ODS Publications, Inc., 444 North Michigan Avenue, Suite 1740, Chicago, Illinois 60611. Licensees may purchase multiple copies of this book at a discount. The book makes an excellent pre-meeting reading assignment and can serve indefinitely as a reference guide.

S A M P L E

LICENSING AGREEMENT

This is to certify that an agreement exists between ODS Publications, Inc. and the Organization known as:

_____
(Your Organization)

Said organization has purchased the right to use the consultant's guides and duplicate the materials described in The Participative Prince by Daniel A. Tagliere, and packaged under the name Organization Development Consultant's Resources.

Purchaser agrees to restrict use to within the organization named above. The transfer of this license is not allowed and the materials may not be duplicated for use in any other organization without written permission of the publisher. Purchase of the licensing agreement in no way permits the purchaser to copy or duplicate the book titled: The Participative Prince.

Date _____   _____SAMPLE ONLY_____
                              For ODS Publications, Inc.

The #100 Series of Resource Materials
and Consultant's Guides

For: Developing individuals to participate more effectively in the organization.

A.   SELF KNOWLEDGE

#101   Self Awareness Exercise
To help individuals "straighten out" their
perceptions, interpretations, feelings, and
intentions regarding major issues and problems in their organization life.

#102   Personal Styles Analyzer
To help individuals become more aware of
their styles in various areas so they are
better prepared to modify them if they
choose.

#103   Participative Proclivities Analyzer/Planner
To help individuals determine the extent
they believe in involving others in their
decisions and how they actually behave.

#104   Work Related Needs Analyzer
To help individuals recognize the relationship between satisfaction of their work
needs and organization performance.

#105   Personal Skills Inventory
To help individuals assess the types and
levels of skills necessary to do their job and
their own levels of competency.

B.   ORGANIZATION GOALS, ROLES AND RESPONSI-
BILITIES

#120   Mission Integration Planner
To help individuals clarify and integrate
their roles with those of the entire organization and the various subunits to which
they belong.

#121   Position Responsibilities Exercise
        To help individuals identify the things they
        should know and be able to do to meet their
        obligations to the organization.

#122   Blank Position Responsibilities Chart
        To provide a format for listing position
        responsibilities.

#123   Work Performance Analyzer
        To help individuals identify how well their
        support, information, training, and motiva-
        tion needs are being met for each of their
        position responsibilities.

#124   Mission, Goals, and Objectives Planner
        To help individuals develop an integrated
        set of long, medium and short range goals.

#125   Performance Objectives Developer
        To help individuals identify, specify, and
        quantify their work goals.

C.   ORGANIZATION RELATIONSHIPS

#140   Organization Position Relationships
        To help individuals identify who they relate
        to in the organization and their interde-
        pendent needs.

#141   Relationships Inventory
        To help people become more aware of their
        organization relationships and form judg-
        ments about modifying them if appropriate.

#142   Interactions Inventory
a & b   To help individuals become more aware of
        how they tend to interact with certain
        individuals or groups and to evaluate the
        results of the present relationship.

#143   Inter-person Work Responsibilities
        To help individuals specify what they need
        from another organization member and
        what the other member needs from them to
        do their respective jobs.

#144   Relationship Profile
        To help individuals analyze a specific rela-
        tionship within the organization.

#145   Machiavellian Matrix
        To help individuals better understand how
        they relate to organization members in
        terms of power.

D. SELF ORGANIZATION

#160   Weekly Time/Activity Log
        To help individuals record and analyze how
        they are now spending their time.

#161   Important/Urgent Exercise
        To help individuals understand the differ-
        ence between important and urgent.

#162   Time/Activity Analyzer
        To help individuals learn how they are
        spending their time in relation to the
        relative importance of the activities that
        make up their jobs.

#163   Decision Making Matrix
        To help individuals systematically deter-
        mine the relative value or most appropriate
        sequence of several choices.

#164   Daily Planner
        To provide individuals with a simple tool
        for planning and scheduling their daily
        activities.

The #200 Series of Resource Materials
and Consultant's Guides

For: Developing Client/Consultant Relationships

#201   Client/Consultant Relationship Description
To help both parties better understand the uniqueness of the client/consultant relationship.

#202   Client/Consultant Meeting Planner
To help both parties plan for their first meeting as client and consultant.

#203   Client/Consultant Exercise
To help both parties illustrate their perception of their relationship and facilitate communication and negotiation.

#204   Client/Consultant Contract Planner
To help both parties prepare to negotiate their relationship roles.

#205   Client/Consultant Relationship Contract
To help both parties express what they will and won't do to make the relationship successful.

#206   Project Profile
To help both parties identify and record basic data on a specific project.

#207   Client Profile
To help the consultant develop basic data on his/her client for initial and reference use.

The #300 Series of Resource Materials
and Consultant's Guides

For: Developing One-on-One Relationships

A.   LEADER/FOLLOWER RELATIONSHIP DEVELOP-
     MENT

 #301 Leader/Follower Development Identifier
    To serve as a cover sheet for the materials
    given to both parties and to specify report-
    ing relationships.

 #302 Summary of the Org Concept
    To provide basic instruction and serve as a
    reference for both parties.

 #303 Leadership Style Guesstimator
    To help the leader and follower identify
    their perceptions of the leader's style.

 #304 Followership Style Guesstimator
    To help both leader and follower identify
    their perceptions of the follower's style.

 #305 The Job Situation Guesstimator
    To help the leader and follower identify
    their perceptions of the follower's job
    situation.

 #306 The Org Report
    To help illustrate both parties' perceptions
    of the entire relationship. This serves as a
    basis for discussion and negotiation.

 #307 Leader/Follower Development Session
    Planner
    To help both parties prepare for a meeting
    to discuss and improve their relationship.

 #308 Leader/Follower Decision Power Specifier
    To help both parties determine the extent
    of their power on issues affecting both.

#309   Leader/Follower Relationship Contract
        To help both parties articulate what they
        will and won't do in the future to make the
        relationship productive and harmonious.

#310   Leader/Follower Relationship Development
a & b   Exercise
        An abbreviated form for helping both par-
        ties understand and discuss their relation-
        ship.

#311   Leader/Follower Position Responsibilities
        Priorities Exercise
        To help structure a discussion between a
        leader and follower about the follower's
        duties and priorities.

B.   OTHER ONE-ON-ONE RELATIONSHIPS

#312   Summary of the Interpersonal Feedback
        Formula
        To help two people discuss emotionally-
        laden issues non-judgmentally. This fosters
        understanding and respect, resolves con-
        flicts, and helps relationships become and
        remain open.

#313   Specialist/User Relationship Exercise
        To help parties in a specialist/user rela-
        tionship to express their perceptions and
        discuss ways to improve the relationship.

#314   Interpersonal Relationship Exercise
        To help the two parties in any relationship
        illustrate their perceptions and feelings
        about the relationship and prepare to dis-
        cuss it.

#315   Interpersonal Role Clarification Exercise
        To help both parties in a relationship
        articulate their views on what both parties
        should be doing for the organization, and to

decide how much time should be spent on each activity.

#316   Other Person's Needs Guesstimator
        To help both parties see each other in terms of work needs, personal needs, and interpersonal needs.

#317   Interpersonal Needs Clarifier
a & b   To help both parties assess their own and the other person's needs from the relationship, and to make judgments regarding the extent the needs are being met.

#318   Relationship Development Planner
        To help parties to a relationship communicate completely about the relationship and make plans for improving it.

C.   RESOLVING INTERPERSONAL CONFLICTS

#350   Conflict Profile
        To help two parties analyze their perceptions of a conflict, articulate their differences, and prepare to resolve it through negotiation.

#351   Conflict Resolution Contract
        To help both parties articulate what they would do and hope the other would do to resolve the conflict.

#352   Conflict Avoidance Planner
        To help both parties identify issues that may develop into a conflict and decide who will make decisions related to these issues.

The #400 Series of Resource Materials
and Consultant's Guides

For: Training and Developing Groups

A.   SELECTION OF GROUP MEMBERS

   #401   Group Member Selection Guide
          To help select the individuals who will be a
          useful resource to the group.

B.   GATHERING DATA AND PREPARING GROUP
     MEMBERS TO PARTICIPATE IN THE GROUP
     DEVELOPMENT EFFORT

   #402   Session Expectations Rater
          To help meeting participants express and
          compare their before and after expecta-
          tions regarding the group development ses-
          sion.

   #403   Group Performance Expectations Rater
          To help group members express their views
          regarding the worthwhileness of the group
          before and after it has been trained and
          developed.

C.   DEVELOPING GROUPS TO MEET INDIVIDUAL
     AND GROUP RELATIONSHIP NEEDS

   #425   The Mission Statement
          To help the group come to a consensus on
          the purpose of the organization or group.

   #426   Problem/Project Prioritization
          To help the group identify the problem/pro-
          jects it will work on and their relative
          importance and urgency.

   #427   Archie Bunker
          To help group members become more sensi-
          tive to stereotypical thinking and the detri-
          mental effect it has on problem solving.

#428   Group Planning
To provide the group with experience in solving a prioritization-type problem alone, democratically, and consensually. Also, to learn a logical planning procedure.

#429   Norm Storming
To help the group become more aware of the influence of norms on their behavior and to help them adopt positive norms.

#430   Organization Interest Groups
To help group members learn about the influence of values on behavior and how their values compare with other group members'.

#431   The Two-Way Communication Exercise
To demonstrate the relative value of one and two way communication and provide a group problem-solving experience.

#432   The Leader/Followers Group Relationship Exercise
To help members of a group, consisting of peers and their leader express their views of the relationships within the group, and improve communications.

#433   The Peer and Mixed Rank Group Relationship Exercise
To help improve relationships within the group.

#434   Objective Setting
To help group members understand the importance and effectiveness of setting specific, attainable, and measurable goals.

#435   Brainstorming
To help group members learn the value and techniques of sustaining judgment and generating large numbers of ideas.

#436 Individual/Group Needs Disclosure
To help group members identify and articulate their needs associated with group
membership.

#437 Individual/Group Contract
To help group members negotiate a
"win/win" contract with the group.

D. TRAINING AND DEVELOPING GROUPS

#450 OD Group-Chairperson's Role

#451 OD Group-Facilitator's Role

#452 Agenda Analysis
To help the group determine what items
should be on their agenda and how they
should be dealt with.

#453-459
To provide individuals and groups with a
logical series of steps to follow when
engaged in various group activities:

#453 Creative Problem Solving Procedure

#454 Corrective Problem Solving Procedure

#455 Preventive Problem Solving Procedure

#456 Project Planning Procedure

#457 Performance or Productivity Improvement
Procedure

#458 Proposal Development Procedure

#459 Proposal Evaluation Procedure

#460 Plan/Solution Evaluator
To help individuals or groups compare the

relative merits of two or more courses of action.

#461   Group and Interpersonal Processes
       To help groups identify helpful and harmful behaviors.

#462   Group Structure Factors and Factual Content Checklist
       To serve as a teaching handout and reference.

#463   Group Problem Solving Performance Rater
       To help a group review its behavior and effectiveness when problem solving and to serve as a basis for improvement.

E.   TRAINING GROUPS TO PLAN AND EXECUTE PROJECTS

#475   Project Factor Evaluation
       To help the members of a task team or project group consider and evaluate the many factors that contribute to the success of a project and to serve as a basis for planning and preparation.

#476   Task Team Member Role Clarifier
       To help the entire task team come to a consensus on what each member will be expected to do and the amount of authority to be given to him or her.

#477   Force Field Analyzer
       To help individuals and groups identify and plan to deal with all the forces that are likely to influence the outcome of a project or decision that may be made.

#478   Group Member Assignments
       To specify what each member of the groups will do for a particular project.

#479 PERT Planner Set
a, b Information and materials to help one or
& c more individuals plan their part in a project
(3 pp) and integrate it into the entire group's
   plans.

#480 Proposal Development and Presentation
   Planner
a, b To help individuals or groups systematically
c & d prepare a proposal in a logical, persuasive
(4 pp) way that facilitates acceptance.

The #500 Series of Resource Materials
and Consultant's Guides

For: Developing a Network of Groups and Intergroup
Relationships

A.   ADMINISTERING THE OD GROUP NETWORK

#501   OD Group Network Planner
To help identify the potential groups in
your organization and to plan for training,
developing and integrating them into the
network.

#502   OD Group Report List
To identify and record the persons in the
organization who should be kept informed
of the group's progress.

#503   OD Group --- Basic Data
To help develop and record the basic facts
about the group's makeup and purpose for
use by members and management.

#504   OD Group Update Information
To provide a systematic way to report
group's area of activities to other groups---
to facilitate intergroup communication.

#505   OD Group Progress Report
To report progress of group on a specific
problem or project.

#506   OD Group Current Assignment of Group
Members
To record what each group member has
agreed to do and the target date.

B. PROMOTING POSITIVE AND PRODUCTIVE RELA-
TIONSHIPS BETWEEN GROUPS IN THE ORGANI-
ZATION

#525 Intergroup Relationships Analyzer
To help group members identify, evaluate
and plan to improve relationships between
their group and other official or unofficial
groups in the organization.

#526 Intergroup Relationship Exercise
To prepare members of two or more groups
to discuss their relationship.

#527 Intergroup Development and Conflict
Resolution Procedure
A step by step procedure for helping two
groups surface their feelings and perceptions about each other and commit to a
positive course of action for both parties
and the organization.

C. MERGING OR COMBINING GROUPS

#540 Group Merger Planner
To help members of a group prepare to
merge with another group.

#541 The Merged Group Constitution
To help the newly formed group gain an
initial cohesiveness through the articula-
tion of its general mission, goals, objectives, structure, and the roles of each
member.

The #600 Series of Resource Materials
and Consultant's Guides

For: Developing Organization Diagnostic Data

A.   DIAGNOSIS --- GATHERING AND INTERPRETING
     DATA

   #601   Mini Organization Needs Survey
          A one-page instrument to help assess the
          adequacy of the factors that influence
          organization success.

   #602   Organization Perceptions Survey and Re-
   (7 pp) sponse Sheet
          A six page survey and separate response
          sheet to help individuals and groups identi-
          fy their perceptions of their organization's
          needs. Used in client/OD consultant rela-
          tionship development, and development of
          high ranking groups as well as general
          diagnostic work.

   #603   Organization Needs Checklist
          A one-page diagnostic tool covering both
          internal and external factors that influence
          organization performance --- to help focus
          efforts for improvement.

   #604   Internal Needs/Performance Rater
          A one page diagnostic tool to help deter-
          mine how the needs of the organization,
          groups, and individuals are being met.

BIBLIOGRAPHY

Argyris, C. Management and Organization Development. New York: McGraw-Hill Book Company, 1971.

Beckhard, R. Organizational Development: Strategies and Models. Cambridge, Mass.: Addison-Wesley, 1969.

Bennis, W. G. Organization Development: Its Nature, Origins and Prospects. Reading, Mass.: Addison-Wesley, 1969.

Blake, R., H. Shepard and J. Mouton. Managing Intergroup Conflict in Industry. Houston: Gulf Publishing, 1964.

Drucker, Peter. Managing for Results. New York: Harper & Row, 1964.

Fordyce, J. K., and R. Weil. Managing with People. Reading, Mass.: Addison-Wesley, 1971.

French, W. L. and Cecil H. Bell, Jr. Organization Development. Englewood Cliffs, N. J.: Prentice Hall, 1973.

Herzberg, F. Work and the Nature of Man. Cleveland, Ohio: World Publications, 1966.

Lawrence, P. R., and J. W. Lorsch. Developing Organizations: Diagnosis and Action. Reading, Mass.: Addison-Wesley, 1969.

Likert, Rensis. The Human Organization: Its Management and Value. New York: McGraw-Hill Book Company, 1967.

Lippitt, G. L. Organization Renewal. New York: Appleton-Century-Crofts, 1969.

Marrow, A. J., D. G. Bowers and S. E. Seashore. Management by Participation. New York: Harper & Row, 1967.

Maslow, A. H. Eupsychian Management. Homewood, Illinois: Richard D. Irwin, Inc., 1965.

McGregor, D. The Human Side of Enterprise. New York: McGraw-Hill Book Company, 1960.

McGregor, D. The Professional Manager. New York: McGraw-Hill Book Company, 1967.

Murray, V. V. "Some Unanswered Questions On Organization Conflict." Organization and Administrative
Sciences. Winter, 1974/75, pp. 35-54.

Robbins, S. P. Managing Organizational Conflict. Englewood Cliffs, N.J.: Prentice Hall, 1974.

Schein, E. H. Process Consultation. Reading, Mass.:
Addison-Wesley, 1969.

Schein, E. H. Process Consultation: Its Role in Organization Development. Reading, Mass.: Addison-
Wesley, 1969.

Seiler, J. A. "Diagnosing Interdepartmental Conflict."
Harvard Business Review. September/October,
1963, pp. 121-132.

Steele, F. I. The Open Organization. Reading, Mass.:
Addison-Wesley, 1975.

Tagliere, D. A. "Organization Development." The
Encyclopedia of Professional Management. New
York: McGraw-Hill Book Company, 1979.

Tagliere, D. A. People, Power and Organization. New
York: AMACOM, 1973.

Tagliere, D. A. "What an Executive Should Know About
Organization Development." A.S.T.D. Journal,
Madison, Wisconsin: July, 1975.

Tagliere, D. A. and F. C. Rebedeau. "Sales Training."
Training and Development Handbook, 2nd Ed. New
York: McGraw-Hill Book Company, 1975.

Tannenbaum, Arnold Sherwood. Social Psychology of the
Work Organization. Belmont, California: Wads-
worth Publishing Co., 1966.

Thomas, John M. and Warren G. Bennis. Management of
Change and Conflict. Baltimore, Md.: Penguin
Books, 1972.

Walton, R. E. Interpersonnel Peacemaking: Confrontation and Third Party Consultation. Reading, Mass.:
Addison-Wesley, 1969.

INDEX